MW00638363

AFRICAN STAR

One Young Man's Voyage of Discovery
A Memoir of 1961

By

E P O'Donnell

BALLYMANUS PRESS

African Star

FIRST EDITION

Library of Congress Cataloging in Publication
Data in Progress

August 2021

To My Wife
Patricia Burns O'Donnell

I am a sailor and you're my first mate;
We signed on together, we coupled our fate;
Hauled up our anchor, determined not to fail,
For the heart's treasure together we set sail.

With no maps to guide us we steered our own course;
Rode out the storms when the winds were gale-force
Sat out the doldrums with patience and hope,
Working together we learned how to cope.

Life is an ocean, and love is a boat,
In troubled waters it keeps us afloat.
When we started the voyage there was just me and you:
Now gathered look around us, we have our own crew.

Together we're in this relationship;
We built it with care to last the whole trip.
Our true destination's not marked on a chart,
We're navigating for the shores of the heart[1].

---

[1] The Voyage, Irish folk song

Contents

Acknowledgements

This book was begun during the dark days of the pandemic when I was forced to abandon other pursuits of a more social nature. For me it was the only good thing to come from this once-in-a-century global scourge so I guess I owe a debt of thanks to the novel Coronanvirus. But I cannot bring myself to do that. Although I am no Anne Frank, that would be like her thanking the Nazis for making her a prisoner so she could write her famous diary.

But I would like to thank my wife Pat for her patience with me and her help and support while I was thus engaged in this mainly solitary literary effort.

My fellow members of Kings Point class of 1964 contributed photos, technical advice and ideas. I was able to draw on them from our lively correspondence in our email group which is a wonderful way for old salts to stay in touch.

Finally I owe a special debt to my own brother Dan for his support and artistic ideas but mainly for going through the manuscript as though it was a Supreme Court brief and finding and correcting my numerous editorial missteps. Only someone who is an accomplished lawyer, actor and playwright could pull that off. Thanks Dan.

Preface

Sixty years have passed since the events in this book took place. I am familiar with them because I was there. The main character is not me, a citizen of very advanced years, but is someone I once was – my eighteen-year-old self. Therefore, I have chosen to write this book not in the first person, as memoirs usually are, but with my younger self set in the third person. Why, you may ask?

The eighteen-year-old who was me no longer exists, except in my memory so he really can't speak to you except through me as narrator. He also did things that I would or could not do now (though I may wish to) so I would like to distance myself from them somewhat. "He" not "I" was responsible – but I do not disavow or deny they happened.

Lastly, he was at the time not aware of the importance of these experiences he went through, and it is only in retrospect that I can see and observe the effects they had on his coming of age.

So this is his story, as told by me, sixty years after he was at a critical point on his journey to manhood and maturity. It is also the story of a bygone era when thousands of American men went to sea in American merchant ships that plied the oceans far and wide. Sadly, that is no longer the reality in 2021, and is but a distant memory.

I hope you will enjoy this retelling of a cadet's first voyage on one of those ships, the African Star, as I did writing about it – and as I did living it.

E P O'Donnell

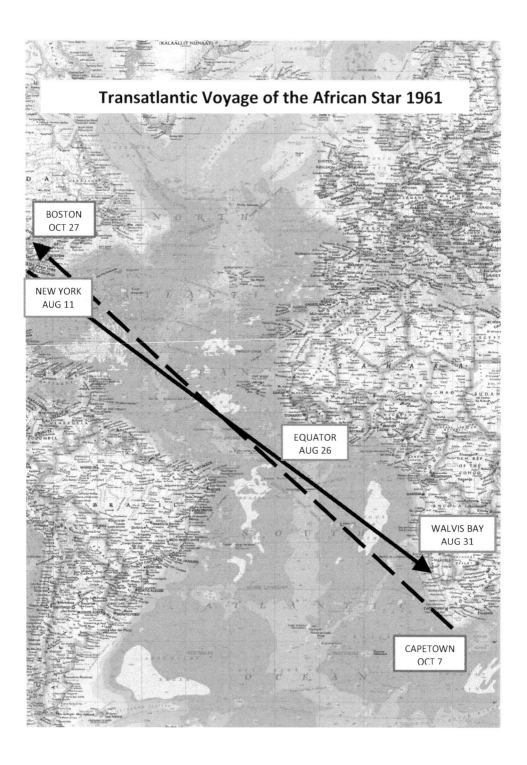

Transatlantic Voyage of the African Star 1961

BOSTON
OCT 27

NEW YORK
AUG 11

EQUATOR
AUG 26

WALVIS BAY
AUG 31

CAPETOWN
OCT 7

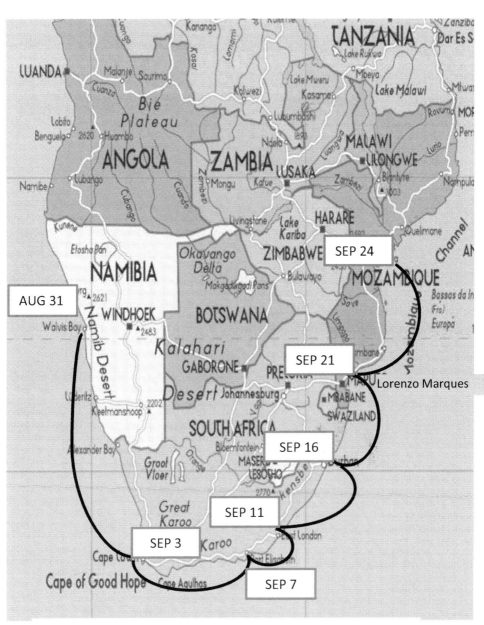

Outbound Ports of Call of African Star 1961

INTRODUCTION

S *ea Year*. The words were a shimmering promise to all plebes. The thought of it helped them endure a long season of confinement and abuse by upperclassmen in 1960-1961 at the US Merchant Marine Academy at Kings Point, New York. It conjured up Joseph Conrad or Herman Melville and the romance and adventure of voyages to distant lands. They would be fulfilling the destiny foretold by the Irish playwright JM Synge that "It's the life of a young man to be going on the sea"[2].

US Merchant Marine Academy Campus, Kings Point

They began the four-year program for creating future merchant marine officers as plebes, with a year of classroom instruction and military discipline. If they survived that, which fully one-third did not, the second was spent as a cadet aboard US merchant vessels plying their trade around the globe. This provided invaluable practical training in the actual work of operating a passenger, cargo or tanker ship. After two more years spent in academic study at the Academy, those who graduated earned the right to serve as licensed deck or engineering officers aboard ship.

They made that choice at the outset. Those with a bent for math often chose engineering. Others wanting to navigate and run cargo operations became deck cadets or "deckies" as they were called. When

---

[2] "Riders to the Sea", John Millington Synge, 1904

Sea Year arrived, each cadet was paired with an opposite number and assigned to a vessel. They shipped out of New York, New Orleans or San Francisco depending on where they lived.

SIGNING ON

"Some years ago, having little in my purse, I thought I would sail about and see the watery part of the world"- Herman Melville

"The gladdest moment in human life, methinks, is a departure to unknown lands" - Sir Richard Burton

As a Staten Island resident Cadet Edward Peter O'Donnell reported, in early August 1961, to Captain Reed, who ran the Academy shipping office on lower Broadway in Manhattan. There he learned his shipmate was to be deck cadet Ron Dreher from Bayonne with whom he would share a cabin on their assigned ship. Eddie knew Ron slightly as he was instrumental in bringing (let's not say procuring) girls from Holy Name Academy, a Catholic girl's high school in Bayonne, NJ to a tea dance at Kings Point during their plebe year. These were highly supervised mixers that eased but not relieved some of the sexual deprivation they endured living like cloistered monks over the long winter months.

Because one of the frequent maritime union strikes threatened to shut down the New York waterfront, O'Donnell and Dreher enjoyed only two weeks at home after plebe year before they received orders to ship out. They were being put on a ship before their promised month long vacation was over.

When they unsealed their orders, they were told to report for a pre-voyage physical at the Farrell Line offices near the Brooklyn piers they operated.

"What's our ship?" Dreher asked.

"It's the SS African Star" O'Donnell read.

"Africa!" exclaimed Ron, "I wanted Europe."

Eddie too was a bit disappointed that his first foreign trip would be to the dark continent instead of a more familiar and popular destination, but he liked the ship's name. African Star. He had to admit it had an allure. Much better than the "Steel Fabricator", a ship his former roommate had gotten.

Farrell Lines, which served West, South and East Africa, named many of its ships with the word "African" paired with a celestial body, hence the "African Moon", "African Sun", etc. Other shipping lines used similar nomenclature. Ithsmian Lines ships were "Steel" combined with occupational names. US Lines also combined "American" with various job titles, as in the "American Flyer" on which Eddie would next serve.

So the two cadets headed out to Brooklyn to have their physicals and get a look at this African Star which would be their home for the next three months. They exited the subway and walked towards the docks though a bustle of trucks and men who were busily engaged in offloading and loading ships tied up along the piers that jutted into New York harbor. They found the Farrell Line office at the head of the company's piers and presented themselves for the routine physicals needed to clear them for the voyage.

Eddie's went without incident as his vital signs and body chemistry were those of a typical eighteen-year old in glowing health. As he waited impatiently for his partner to complete his and join him to go aboard the ship, there appeared a crestfallen Dreher. He informed O'Donnell that the doctor had diagnosed a hernia that was judged too risky to release him for a voyage aboard a company vessel with no doctor or trained medical staff.

One might suspect that the company viewed cadets as non-essential crew members who did not warrant assumption of any added liability – they were not cargo that would pay its own way.

When informed of this development by phone, Captain Reed said he had no choice but to pull Ron off any ship until he had the hernia fixed[3]. Reed told O'Donnell that there was no time to find a replacement deck cadet as the ship was sailing the next day. Eddie would have to sail solo.

---

[3]While dealing with this, Dreher opted to switch from deck to engine and thus had to repeat plebe year, albeit it with the privileges of an upperclassman. Thus his hernia allowed him to redirect his career before his sea year.

So he reluctantly parted ways with Ron and went alone to go aboard and introduce himself to the Chief Engineer who would oversee his training, at least nominally. As Eddie approached the ship, the words African Star stood out far above him on the bow in block letters above the black hull. The ship's stack bore the Farrell Lines house flag insignia. She was about 500 feet in length and was launched in 1946 so she was in the middle of her useful life as a general cargo vessel.

SS African Star Underway

She was one of 465 ships designated as C-3 and built by the US Maritime Commission during and shorty after WWII. As Eddie passed down her length to the midships gangway, he could see pallets of manufactured goods and equipment being raised on large cargo booms to be lowered into her three holds forward and two holds aft of her midship superstructure that held the crew quarters and navigation bridge.

He climbed the gangway and was directed up to the officers' quarters where he found the Chief's office. His greeting was rather brusque and he told Eddie to see the Purser about his cabin and then go below to the engine room where he could find the First Assistant Engineer who would tell him what to do.

The Purser turned out to be more welcoming as he gave the cadet a key to the cabin which was in fact right next door to the Chief Engineer's. Eddie entered and found a room with bunk beds, table which doubled as a desk in front of a built-in settee and a small sink under a medicine cabinet. It also had a private toilet and shower. A porthole opened onto the promenade deck just outside.

'Not a bad setup' he thought, 'particularly since I have it all to myself.'

He changed from his tan summer service uniform into more informal khakis and short sleeve shirt with epaulets displaying his rank as cadet third class (i.e., sophomore). He put on his military high pressure hat and went out to find the engine room and the First Assistant Engineer.

A word is in order about ranks aboard a US merchant ship. Since man began venturing to sea the undisputed head of any vessel has been known as the Master or Captain of the ship. In the age of sail, he was assisted by one or more officers of the deck called mates, ranked first (or chief), second and third. When steam power replaced sail, more specialized officers were needed to tend to the propulsion plant. These became the engineers - the chief, and his assistants first, second and third.

The Captain and Chief Engineer each are entitled to wear four stripes, implying an equality of rank, but the Captain is the first among equals. His license in fact names him Master as in days of old. The First Mate and First Assistant Engineer are three stripers and so on down the ranks to the lowly Third Mate and Third Assistant Engineers who merit a single stripe much like a naval Ensign.

From this one would think that officer dress aboard a merchant ship would be like that aboard a naval warship – everyone decked out in their uniforms with insignia of rank proudly displayed. But, as Eddie quickly learned – you would be wrong. Other than the Captain and Chief Engineer, virtually no one else wore stripes or even a uniform. The common form of dress was khakis, but not always. Work clothes of all sorts, boiler suits, dungarees and plain civilian garb were the order of the day.

When Eddie first appeared below, he found John Leslie, The First Assistant Engineer, who was engaged in supervising work on a large pump. He took one look at Eddie and said "Gadget, you can't do anything useful in that getup. Go put on your dungarees and get back down here."

From upperclassmen who had been to sea, Eddie knew that "Gadget" was a term of either endearment or scorn, depending on the user's point of view, applied to Kings Pointers aboard ship by the seasoned hands. It was an obvious and intentional corruption of the word "Cadet" and implied either a somewhat limited usefulness, or a shiny object of dubious value. Eddie's uniformed appearance put him in the latter category where he would remain unless and until he proved otherwise.

He quickly went back to his cabin and changed into his academy-issue denim work uniform and reported again to the First. Leslie was an older man, seeming then to Eddie ancient, but he was in fact about sixty – thin, balding and bespectacled. He was overseeing a group of men who were trying to mount a large motor in place atop a pump.

"Now jumBO, heave left!" he yelled to a man who was positioned below the deck plates on which they were all standing. This individual pushed the large motor which was suspended from a chain fall into the exact position to enable another worker to line up holes on a flange and insert bolts to couple the pump and motor together.

After they completed the job, Eddie saw emerge from below a mountain of a man with the stub of a cigar in his clenched teeth which were surrounded by a scruffy growth of facial hair. He was a light skinned man of color with an enormous girth who gave the cadet a wide grin.

"This is our new gadget, Jumbo", said the First by way of introductions.

'So that was his name!' Eddie thought. 'I thought he said "Jimbo"', which was what his Uncle Dan Duffy, himself a former merchant mariner, called Eddie's brother Jim. Considering the size of the man, Jumbo made far more sense. He grasped the cadet's extended fingers in his catcher's mitt of a hand and welcomed him aboard.

Eddie soon learned that Jumbo was the lead wiper in the "black gang" as the engine crew were known. A wiper is the lowest rating in the engine room and as the name implies, the job involved cleaning spills, painting, general housekeeping and brute labor[4]. Besides the three wipers and the six licensed engineers, the rest of the black gang consisted of two electricians (Chief and Second), three oilers who monitored the machinery and three firemen who tended the ship's boilers. Eddie got to know these men and their respective roles in the scheme of things quite well over the coming days aboard the ship.

He also got introductions to the Second Assistant Engineer Andy Anderson and the three Thirds, named White, Rizzo and Decker. As the ship was in port, all were in the engine room getting the machinery in

---

[4]One of the plebe year instructors was referred to by the cadets as Joe the Wiper. He lacked a degree or good command of engineering theory but was very adept at the practical side of things.

good working order for a three-month voyage which would depend on their skill in operating and maintaining it.

After the pump work was completed, it was time to knock off for lunch and White and Rizzo offered to treat the new cadet to lunch ashore rather than eating aboard in the officers dining room. Eddie didn't want to appear standoffish so agreed to take them up on the invitation.

The three debarked to a diner just off the piers. Eddie soon understood the reason for their choice of venue. The diner had a fully stocked bar while the ship was a dry hole – no alcohol allowed on board, at least not in plain sight. Not wanting to appear stiff with these potential useful sources of arcane engineering knowledge, Eddie ordered a beer as he was in fact of legal drinking age, at that time eighteen in New York state. Food was also ordered but this clearly was an afterthought for their primarily liquid lunch.

By way of conversation Eddie asked, "So how long have you been aboard the African Star?"

"Two days", laughed Rizzo as White nodded. Seeing Eddie's puzzled look, they said "we're relief engineers signed on for just one voyage, filling in for the permanent Thirds and so is Decker. The Chief, First and Andy are lifers."

So here was the first inkling of a fault line that would later emerge between the more established and the transient members of the engineering staff. Eddie instinctively recognized that he had best avoid too close a relationship with this unmoored relief faction and instead seek the guidance and approval of the establishment figures who in any case were the senior officers in his department. No rebel with or without a cause was he.

This situation reflected the structure then in place aboard American flagged ships which were organized under a labyrinth of labor agreements. Each department had its own union. The engineers belonged to the Marine Engineers Beneficial Association (MEBA) which sounds like a benevolent charity or an insurance company. It was instead the oldest maritime trade union formed in 1875 to represent engineers aboard early American steamships. It's leader in 1961 was one Jessie Calhoon, a hard-nosed bargainer. All engineers, including Eddie upon graduation would have to be dues paying MEBA members in order to work aboard most US ships.

The deck officers were represented by the Masters, Mates and Pilots (MM&P) union (which MEBA members often referred to as the Masturbating Pilots). Crew members below decks had to join one of two unions. The largest was the National Maritime Union (NMU) which represented engine, deck and steward's department members in most Atlantic and Pacific coast ports. Ships operating from southern and gulf ports had crews supplied by the Seafarers International Union (SIU).

There was no love lost between these two rival unions. SIU members were mainly southern whites who often referred to their NMU brethren as "N_____s, Misfits and Undesirables". In this pre-civil rights era, such pronouncements often elicited chuckles rather than outrage. Such was the degree of solidarity among the maritime unions, all of which co-existed under the AFL-CIO labor umbrella.

The terms of union agreements generally extended for several years but had different expiration dates. So as each union came to the table to seek more pay and benefits, a strike was possible any time a dispute became intractable. Added to this was the labor power of the longshoremen's and teamsters' unions which could also bring port operations to a halt with a strike every few years. This hodgepodge of unions was the bane of the shipping line operators which had to separately deal with each in turn. The result was frequent forced shutdowns, one of which loomed over the African Star as it loaded for departure in August 1961, and was the reason for Eddie's shortened summer vacation and reluctant orders to proceed without a deck cadet as a companion on his maiden voyage.

The division between permanent and relief crew members reflected the structure of the various sea going union contracts. To get a berth aboard a ship, engineers, mates or crew members went to their respective union halls in each port where available jobs were posted for bidding by the members. Jobs were either permanent, enabling one to remain with that ship as long as one pleased, or they were relief jobs – good for one voyage only as you were filling in for a permanent crew member who was entitled to leave or vacation but still had claim to a permanent berth.

Some ships were highly desirable because of their routes or physical attributes or company reputation. A key factor was the quality of food which seasoned hands could rate as though they were awarding Michelin stars to Parisian bistros. The highest acclaim afforded a ship's cuisine was to say "She's a Feeder". A Feeder with a good itinerary of ports and a benevolent shipping company operator was a "Home". Many of the

Farrell Line ships (though not those serving West Africa) were in this category and staffed by "lifers", men holding permanent berths for years on end, only leaving the ship for a vacation when necessary.

Members bidding on open jobs had priority based on how long they had been "on the beach". They were assigned a number when they first registered for employment and the longer they went without using it, their place in the bidding queue improved with age. In good economic times with many jobs available, a man could land a choice permanent job with a fairly low priority number. In lean times, competition was fierce and it could be a long time before a plum berth came his way.

So it was just happenstance that all three of the African Star's permanent Thirds were being replaced on this voyage by three relief engineers. After Eddie's lubricated lunch with two of them which, in the sixty minutes available, left none of them the worse for wear, they returned to the ship for the remainder of the workday which ended promptly at 5 p.m. per the union contract. Mr. Leslie told the cadet he was free to go but must report back for duty next day at 8 a.m. prepared to leave with the ship later that day. It was to be Eddie's last night as a landlubber.

TAKING LEAVE

He had carefully laid his plans for his leave taking from hearth and home. Of course he would have a farewell dinner with his family. But his remaining moments would be shared with Sophie Stefanski his girlfriend of almost two years. Their relationship had begun at the very start of Eddie's senior year at St Peter's Boys High School. He had heard of this Polish-born girl who was a sophomore at St Peter's Girls High School but had never laid eyes on her until he was introduced to her by his good friend Dick Kennedy who had brought her as his date to a dance at their parish church. This proved an unfortunate move for Dick, as there was an instant and electric field of attraction between Sophie and Eddie. He asked her to dance and their first physical contact confirmed what their eyes were telling them – it was in truth love at first sight.

She was not Eddie's normal type which tended to be dark haired blue eyed girls with fair complexions. An Irish archetype in other words. Sophie had striking hazel eyes and medium brown luxuriant hair that was her pride and joy. She was not tall, only 5'2" or so but well proportioned, with curves in all the right places. Her mouth was ever so slightly crooked which strangely enough added to her allure as it was very expressive and sensuous. She was like a Slavic princess, and he was ready to abandon his Celtic preferences in order to seek her favor.

After their fateful but brief meeting, Eddie thought a great deal about her during the following days but was resigned to the awkward fact that she was with his friend Dick. Besides, Eddie was extremely shy with girls at that age and had failed to act on several crushes he had on girls that would probably have welcomed his attentions.

But Sophie was not like other girls. She had been born in 1944 in Nazi Germany of Polish parents who were enforced laborers of the Third Reich[5]. Her unauthorized birth itself had to be initially hidden from the authorities who may have removed her or worse if discovered. This harrowing experience forged a bond between Sophie and her parents that was as strong as the force which holds particles in the nucleus of an atom together. She would be an only child which allowed father and mother to lavish all their love and devotion on her.

This small nuclear Stefanski family survived the war and six years in a refugee camp before gaining their freedom and emigrating to America

---

[5] At some point she showed Eddie her original birth certificate that horrifyingly bore a large swastika.

in 1951. So Sophie arrived in Staten Island as a seven-year old waif speaking no English. The family settled in a section of Staten Island centered on St Adalbert's Polish church. Sophie's native intelligence came to the fore as she quickly learned English from the nuns which she then proceeded to teach her parents.

So this Polish immigrant, now a stunning fifteen-year old took matters into her own hands where Eddie was concerned. At a dance the next Friday at St Peter's, she immediately made a bee line towards him and proceeded to flirt in a very open manner. It was no contest. He was an older man of sixteen but hers for the taking and take she did. Before the very chagrined eyes of Dick Kennedy, Sophie and Eddie became an item.

To an observer Dick had it all: good looks, athletic prowess, popularity, great clothes (his father owned an upscale men's shop) and money. But he could not keep the only thing of his that Eddie really wanted. However improbably, he, not Dick, was Sophie's Choice.

The relationship developed and continued through Eddie's senior year and plebe year at Kings Point, surviving a number of ups and downs of spats, separations and happy reunions. As he now prepared to leave for darkest Africa they were in a good phase, and her mother had treated them the tickets to see *Ben Hur* at the Ritz, the local movie theater which was then showing that great classic.

While they were absorbed in the action on screen for a time, their closeness and the knowledge that this was their last date soon gave way to what Sophie would call a "PDA", which she normally disdained. In the darkened balcony, their display of mutual affection was not really a public one, so no objections were raised.

They parted tearfully in the wee hours of the night with mutual promises to write and maintain fidelity during their forced separation. Eddie was concerned that Sophie would be sorely tempted by many suitors during her own senior year of high school. She was a popular, attractive seventeen-year old cheerleader who almost any boy would kill to date. He had visions of joining Dick Kennedy on the ash heap of her discarded boyfriends. But little did Eddie then realize that he would be the one to betray her.

After a few hours' sleep, he bid farewell to his parents and with packed bags found his way back to Brooklyn and his new floating home. His dear mother had freshly laundered and packed his clothes and essentials for the trip. At the Academy civilian clothes were forbidden, but for sea duty they were not only permitted but highly recommended for shore leave. In this cold war era, it was considered inadvisable to go ashore in a US uniform of any sort – not forbidden, just a cautious practice in case you were in a place where American servicemen could be targeted.

During the day Eddie assisted the engineers in preparing the African Star for departure that evening. This involved topping off fuel oil bunkers, taking on stores and spare parts and finishing any remaining maintenance work in the engine room. As a green cadet he was charged with fetching tools, stowing parts and being a courier as needed. He had his first meals aboard the ship in the engineers' mess where one ordered from a daily menu which offered several choices at each meal. They were served by a mess room waiter, a member of the stewards department overseen by the Purser.

This group included cooks, dishwashers, waiters and general housekeepers who daily cleaned the officers' (but not cadets') staterooms. As their duties involved no special nautical skills (unless you count the occasional need to cook and serve meals during a typhoon), they were not held in high esteem by the deck or engine crew members. But these were good paying union jobs so they were hard to come by and any "misfits or undesirables" were soon sent packing. Eddie came to know and respect most of the stewards during the voyage.

In anticipation of an evening departure, at noon the ship's work routine was transformed to that observed at sea. This involved setting of watches in the engine room and on the bridge. At sea, the day was divided into six four watch periods. The Third Mates and Engineers assumed the duty of overseeing operations above and below decks on a four hour on, eight hour off routine. Those on the 8-12 watch had the most "normal" work schedule. They were roused for breakfast at 7:15 a.m. before reporting for duty at the stroke of 8 a.m. At noon they were relieved and were free until 8 p.m. when they resumed their watch duty until midnight when they could then get a full night's sleep until called again.

The 4-8 and 12-4 watches followed the same routine for those hours. Watch standers worked seven days a week. Those who did not stand watch were considered "day" workers, with an 8 a.m.–5 p.m. schedule, including a one-hour lunch period. Day workers had weekends off unless overtime was scheduled.

A cadet's normal schedule coincided with the First and Second engineers and the wipers who were also day workers. Thus Eddie came to know Leslie, Andy and Jumbo quite well. At times he would be put on a rotating watch schedule to learn the duties of a Third Assistant Engineer. This became his main source of interactions with White, Rizzo and Decker, the relief engineers.

As the ship was due to sail at 8 p.m., Eddie was told to knock off at noon, but directed by the First to report to the engine room at 7 p.m. to assist with and observe maneuvering operations below. A steamship is a very complex organism from an engineering perspective, particularly one designed in the 1940s, with very little automation. During maneuvering, when the ship is moving from the dock and getting underway, the steam plant must respond to various bell commands from the bridge which are communicated via the engine room telegraph.

Engine Room Telegraph

Anyone who has seen "Titanic" will recognize this as the brass-handled device through which the mate on watch tried to get the ship to go from "Full Ahead" to "All Stop" to "Full Astern" to avoid the ship's fatal encounter with the iceberg at 2 a.m. What is unseen is that these bell commands are relayed below and answered by the engine room which must control the propulsion turbine to change the ship's speed and direction on command.

Going from dock to open sea rarely involves such drastic maneuvers as the Titanic required, but it is a time when things can go very wrong with serious consequences. For this reason, the First Assistant Engineer takes control of things from the watch engineer during maneuvering operations. On the bridge, a harbor pilot who knows the local waterways and navigational procedures like no else, is in command.

§●§ ●§● § ●§

When Eddie got to the engine room at 7 p.m., Leslie was already there directing things and warming up the turbines in readiness for getting underway. Because Decker, the Third on watch was new to the ship as was the fireman, Andy the Second Engineer was also there to assist. The oiler on watch rounded out the team.

There was an air of tension and anticipation that was absent earlier in the day. They were going to sea!

Actually they were going to Newark. Before heading out the Narrows to the broad Atlantic and a southbound course for Africa, they had to sail down the Kill Van Kull, the shipping channel between Staten Island and New Jersey, to load some deck cargo in Port Newark. This would consume the rest of the 8-12 watch and it would be well into the start of the new day before the ship dropped the pilot and was on its own.

The First advised the cadet that his role in all this would be rather simple: man the telegraph and keep the bell log. Shortly after 8 p.m. the telegraph sprang to life as the bridge signaled Slow Astern. Eddie moved the handle to acknowledge receipt and recorded the command and time in a log book. The First turned a large throttle valve to admit steam to the astern turbine. The fireman and engineers increased the firing rate on the boilers to meet the steam demand. The oiler made sure the feed pumps kept up with the boilers' greater thirst for water.

As the turbines responded, Eddie could see on the very rudimentary control panel that the propeller shaft began turning slowly in a reverse direction and he could feel the ship inching away from the pier.

Steamship Engine Room Control Panel[6]

---

[6] Photo compliments of Bill Long USMMA Class of 1964

15

As they moved out into the harbor, the telegraph rang with increasing frequency as the ship gained speed and moved towards its destination. The new cadet was mesmerized. It was a finely choreographed dance of men and machines that was fascinating to watch – much more so because it entirely involved human interactions and communication. No computers. No glowing screens.

This process of maneuvering continued for the next few hours as the ship went from Brooklyn to Port Newark, docked again briefly and then resumed its way back down the Kill Van Kull towards the Narrows and open water. A little past midnight the First told Eddie he was free to leave as the oiler would take over the bell log. He was eager to go topside to see just where they were so Eddie took him up on his offer.

As he came up on deck he could see it was a clear, quiet moonlit summer night. Then he recognized a very familiar sight. They were just about to pass under the Bayonne Bridge. His immediate thoughts turned to Sophie whose house was in the shadow of the bridge which they often strolled across together. A pang of longing hit him, knowing she was probably sleeping, dreaming just a few hundred yards away. The ship passed silently under the bridge and Eddie looked straight down her street and saw her slumbering form in his mind's eye.

As he watched the Staten Island shore glide by, he could see other familiar landmarks: Weissglass Stadium, the scene of popular stock car races; the PAL center where he first played organized basketball, and the American Legion hall where, as a ten-year-old, he attended a screening of Victory at Sea which stirred him to the core.

Then Eddie realized he could soon also look down Pelton Avenue where his own family would be fast asleep. The white-washed form of the historic Pelton House at the start of the street appeared ahead, which was his cue to gaze intently down the dimly lit lane he knew so well. It was almost surreal to think that here he was and there his brothers Dan and Jim and sister Sheila and mom and dad were. They were in such proximity but in different worlds. At dawn they would go about their lives with no great change in familiar routines, while Eddie would begin a journey into a life completely new.

Soon after Pelton Avenue the ship passed by Sailors' Snug Harbor which fronted the Kill Van Kull a short distance from Eddie's house. It had been established in 1833 as a home for retired seamen with buildings in the Greek revival style. It covered some 83 acres and during the 1950s it also included a working farm with livestock and horses. As a boy Eddie and his friends would sneak onto the property to ride the horses and run from the bull who sometimes charged the intruders. It was as though they were Kansas farm boys rather than New York City residents. As the ship passed by Eddie smiled at the memory of it as well as his father's joking comment that, as a seagoing man himself now, Eddie was assured of a place in Snug Harbor when the time came.

Soon the African Star entered the harbor and turned towards the Narrows. Eddie decided to call it a night. As he walked to his solitary room, he was hit with waves of conflicting emotion and realized that he was exhausted from the day's events. He managed to put his head on the pillow and eventually drift off to sleep, mercifully undisturbed by dreams of any kind.

UNDERWAY

He was awakened by the sound of bells. Bong-bong, bong-bong. Four bells. His mind pondered this strange sound. Four bells again. Eddie sat up rubbing the sleep from his eyes and remembered where he was.

'Oh yeah. Four bells, in two pairs. On a ship that means the middle of the watch, now the morning watch. Ten am. I missed breakfast and, Christ! Late for work. Wait. it's Saturday. No work on the weekend for day workers like me. Well that's a relief'. He felt the rhythmic motion of the ship as she plowed through the water.

He arose and dressed and went out into the passageway leading to the promenade deck outside the engineers' quarters. He stepped out into the morning sunlight and breathed in the air, salt air like he had never smelt or tasted before. He looked aft and saw the ship's foamy wake churning and spreading out behind the ship. Eddie's gaze extended to and swept the horizon in search of — land. But there was none. For the first time in his life he was beyond the view of terra firma. No beach, no hill, no tree, no blade of grass in sight.

'Well' he thought, 'now you've done it - you're at sea. Are you happy now?'

Actually he was. Eddie was thrilled to think that he was now in the company of generations of the seagoing Irish men of Arran and his parents' native Donegal – he was young and was "on the sea".

He was also hungry so he made his way to the engineer's mess in search of something to eat and drink. There sat the First and Andy, the Second Engineer, having a mid-morning coffee break.

"Well Gadget, I can see you're no early bird", said Leslie with a hint of disapproval. Eddie said he hadn't set an alarm so had no idea what time it was until he awoke.

"You missed breakfast but there's coffee there and you can make toast if you like" Andy offered. "There's nothing in the fridge but the usual – cheese and horse cock."

"What?" Eddie said "Did you say horse cock?"

They laughed and Andy went to the small fridge and took out a plate bearing a length of thick sausage and Eddie grasped his meaning.

"You will find this in on every ship in every fridge and night lunch", he explained.

"If you're hungry enough it makes a decent snack with plenty of mustard, but I try never to get that hungry.'

Andy was a pudgy man with a fringe of reddish hair surrounding his bald pate. He didn't look like he experienced hunger pangs or the soreness that comes with vigorous exercise very often. But he was a jovial sort who was glad to help a new cadet learn the ropes of the seafaring life.

Eddie helped himself to coffee and the First said there was fresh milk which Eddie poured in liberally along with his usual two packets of sugar. It was sweet coffee but it was the only way he could drink it.

"Enjoy the milk while you can, it won't last long" said Leslie.

"And tonight's steak and salad night" Andy added.

They explained that the best food and meals aboard ship were those served up in the days after sailing. The store of perishable items would be expended in about a week, so that on a long voyage like this one, dairy products and fresh vegetables which had a limited shelf life were nowhere to be found for most of the trip until reaching port where they could be replenished.

"When will we get to port?" Eddie asked.

"Had enough sea time already?" laughed Leslie.

"No, not at all, just curious", Eddie said somewhat defensively.

"We'll be in Walvis Bay in about three weeks" he advised, referring to the ship's first scheduled stop on the African coast.

"I think he's a shore hound", Andy teased.

This Eddie learned was a derisive term applied to crew members who queued up in their best clothes at the gangway as a ship was docking at a new port, eager to rush ashore to the fleshpots that just as eagerly awaited them and their money.

While Eddie wasn't yet dying to set foot ashore, he imagined three weeks at sea could transform one into a shore hound quite readily, but he resolved to not acquire that sort of reputation when the time came.

'Play it cool', he thought.

This trip did turn out to be the longest stretch of sea time Eddie experienced during his time spent aboard ships, but it was the most pleasant and uneventful weather-wise. The Captain had set a southeast course which would take them down the broad Atlantic, bound for the southwest coast of Africa. The voyage of more than 7,000 miles would take about 20 days at the 15 knot cruising speed of the vessel. Weather was an unknown factor of course, but they were in the sweet spot as far as that was concerned.

Leaving New York in late summer meant they were moving towards the equator as the seasons were reversing in the hemispheres it delineated. The ship would reach that imaginary line in about two weeks, in late August, just before the onset of the southern spring. Thus the balance of the voyage would be spent in waters and weather that were emerging from winter towards a warmer seasonal climate in the south. They would return to New York in late October well before northern winter had set in.

As a result, although Eddie had not yet gotten his sea legs, there would be no episodes of seasickness or motion sickness to which he was sometimes prone. He would be sorely put to the test on his next ship, the American Flyer, which had to make two crossings of the stormy north Atlantic in the dead of winter. Until then he would remain serenely oblivious to what bad weather could do a ship at sea.

The two engineers finished their coffee break and Leslie told Eddie he was free to do as he liked for the weekend but advised that it would be a good opportunity to explore the ship and familiarize himself with the engine room where he would be mainly working. The cadet told him he would do just that right after lunch.

He returned to his cabin and began organizing his little world. Clothes were neatly stowed in drawer and closet, toiletries laid out and his desk organized. While learning how theory was put into practice aboard ship, cadets were expected to complete written assignments which demonstrated that knowledge. Reports and drawings were required on all facets of the ship's design and operations. Besides these technical subjects, the humanities were not ignored. Cadets were given reading assignments and supplied with a selection of books which were required to be read and critiqued in book reports.

These assignments were set forth in a three ring binder known as the Sea Project. During sea year cadets were expected to complete and periodically mail in various sections for grading. Failure to do so, or bad grades, could result in expulsion from the Academy. The Sea Project wasn't that difficult but it required work and discipline to keep up with it. A few cadets found themselves back in civilian life because they failed to take care of this business. Perhaps they were shore hounds or just lazy but their excuses fell on deaf ears.

Eddie diligently began to lay out his Sea Project assignments, one of which was to complete data sheets on the ship's engine machinery. The First told him the Chief Engineer had in his office all the required drawings and specifications Eddie would need. After lunch, he meekly knocked on his door which was open. Eddie had had no real interaction as yet with this man who was in overall charge of things in the department. His name was Rommel as the cadet determined from his license which was prominently displayed along with that of all the officers on a bulkhead as required by the Coast Guard.

He was a fit looking man of medium height in his mid-fifties with steel gray hair and a somewhat sallow complexion. He did not exude a friendly vibe and responded to Eddie's request by pointing to a set of file cabinets that containing what he desired.

"Take what you need, but put them back where you found them", he directed.

The art of small talk was clearly not his strong suit so Eddie quickly gathered up an armful of documents and retreated to his cabin next door.

'Boy', Eddie thought, 'he's a tough cookie'. He mused whether the Chief was related to the Desert Fox, Erwin Rommel, as Eddie imagined that the famous Nazi general would display a similar icy demeanor to his subordinates. He later came to understand that the Chief was one of those old seadogs who viewed Kings Point cadets and graduates as pampered, overeducated individuals taking the places of more deserving men who "came up the hawsepipe" – a term denoting officers who rose from the ranks, much as an anchor is raised up through the opening in the bow – the hawsepipe.

TOPSIDE

Eddie spent the rest of the day exploring the confines of the 500 ft. piece of floating real estate that was carrying him and about fifty other souls across a vast ocean. He began at the top, climbing stairs up to the bridge. Eddie entered from the portside wing bridge and introduced himself to the Third Mate on watch who apparently knew the story of the missing deckie.

"Hello cadet, I'm John Wheaton. Sorry your partner got shanghaied. I don't know much about engines but I can fill you in on what goes on up here".

He was a handsome young guy in his early thirties dressed in crisp khakis though without sign of rank. He introduced Eddie to the seaman who was standing at the ship's steering station which was a stand with a spoked wheel. It was from here the massive rudder at the stern could be controlled to change course. It contained a compass that displayed the ship's heading which Eddie could see was towards the southeast.

Navigation Bridge (Liberty Ship)

Engine cadets had taken a basic navigation course and Eddie was interested in this. He asked Wheaton about how he could tell where the ship was with no landmarks in sight.

"Well we really don't. We just go until we bump into land", joked the mate.

Wheaton then took him into the chart room and showed him their projected course to Africa.

"We're following a great circle route", referring to the shortest path between New York and Walvis Bay – along a global circumference.

23

Wheaton then explained that they tried to establish their exact position each day by "shooting the sun" at noon to find the ship's latitude and by "shooting the stars" at night to get their longitude. In this pre-GPS age celestial navigation was the only reliable means of establishing a ship's deep sea location, just as in the days of Columbus.

"What if it's cloudy or we're fogged in?" Eddie asked the mate.

"Then we use dead reckoning", he replied.

Even engine cadets knew this referred to estimating how far the ship had travelled from its last known position based on the ship's estimated speed and course.

"It's called that because you can be dead wrong" Wheaton said with a smile.

"A ship doesn't have a speedometer and how fast we're actually going depends a lot on the weather conditions. And although we think we know the direction we're heading, the current can take us off course very easily, especially as we're crossing the Gulf stream which takes everything to the northeast. I'm always glad when we can get a fix on our position from the sun and stars".

As this point Wheaton turned to greet a man who had come onto the bridge from the aft passageway.

"Afternoon skipper", he said.

"Same to you Wheaton. Who have we here?"

This was Eddie's first encounter with Captain James Farnsworth. The mate introduced Eddie and Farnsworth said "Happy to have you aboard O'Donnell. No U-boats to worry about like in my sea year."

Farnsworth was a Kings Point grad class of '46. He and other cadets who went through the Academy in WWII served aboard ships during the Battle of the Atlantic when German submarines sunk 1555 US merchant ships with the loss of thousands of lives. Serving on a merchant ship was especially dangerous during what the Nazi submariners called their "Happy Time", when they could sink ships with impunity in 1942-43, even in American waters within sight of the east coast.

The ship was actually the second Farrell ship with that name. The original African Star had been hit by a German torpedo in the South Atlantic in 1943. Because at this time the Nazis were still playing nice, they allowed the crew to abandon ship before they sent her to the bottom with a second torpedo. As a result, she lost only one of her crew who had been blown overboard when the first fish struck.

After convoys with naval escorts were instituted, sinkings like this became less frequent but serving on a merchant ship remained a hazardous assignment and the U boats gave no quarter if they could find a target. They would make sure it went down with all hands.

During the war, 142 cadets were lost at sea in the line of duty. At first, the names of the fallen were commemorated on the mess hall wall at Kings Point but, as the losses mounted and the list grew long, this memorial was covered up to avoid demoralizing those who were yet to go to sea. This hidden memorial was only recently re-discovered and is now a shrine to "The 142" and an inspiration to cadets who take their meals today in the mess hall.

Farnsworth looked out the bridge window and borrowed a set of binoculars from the mate. He scanned the starboard horizon and said to Wheaton, "Is that one of ours?" the captain asked, pointing out a ship far off to the southwest.

"We picked her up on radar at the start of the watch. Sparky says it's the Sun homeward bound".

"Cadet go tell Sparks to send her my greetings and to splice the main brace", Farnsworth said to Eddie.

Seeing the cadet's puzzled look he translated, "Go into the radio shack just down the passageway and ask the Radio Officer to send a welcome home message to Captain Simmons of the African Sun which is that ship over there. Tell him to have a drink on me after he docks."

Eddie obediently if uncertainly proceeded down the passageway where he found a room with a short, bald older man sitting hunched over in front of a large wireless set tapping out Morse code on a key pad. Seeing Eddie, he stopped and removed his headphones.

"Vas is up?" he said in a German sounding accent. Eddie relayed the message from the captain.

This was Ronald Klouters, known as "Sparks", the term applied to Radio Officers on all merchant ships. These individuals filled an important role as they were the sole communication link with the outside world when a ship was at sea. News, company instructions and, most importantly, weather reports, came in over the long distance short wave radio. In those days these messages were in Morse code.

On a cargo ship like the African Star there was only a single Radio Officer and the solitary nature of their job, listening intently to dots and dashes coming through the ether, set them apart from the other officers. In short, they were a strange lot, and Klouters was no exception. He was

25

an older man, maybe in his mid-sixties. His accent was not German, but Afrikaans which was an official language of South Africa then, besides English.

Sparks was a native South African, a descendant of the Boer farmers who had first settled the area and had fought a nasty little colonial war with the British Empire at the turn of the twentieth century. The Boers lost the war but emerged as equal partners in ruling the land and its native population over most of the century.

Klouters had a family that lived in Pietermaritzburg, a pretty mountain town between Capetown and Durban. It was the capital of Natal province.

"Vait till you get to Capetown cadet, you will find plenty of good beer and in Durban you will find plenty of pretty girls".

Eddie took note of this sage advice. Klouters was a man who looked a bit like Yoda, teacher of Luke Skywalker. Surely he spoke the truth on these two matters of great interest to Eddie and indeed, as it turned out, he did.

Eddie left Sparks to his dits and dahs and passed through the main dining room where the Captain, Chief Engineer and mates took their meals. He was also entitled to dine there as were the other engineers, but Eddie invariably chose the more relaxed atmosphere of the engineers' mess room for his meals.

Adjacent to the dining room were a number of passenger cabins, currently unoccupied. Cargo ships like the African Star could carry up to twelve paying passengers. Beyond this number a ship was required to have a doctor on board as was the case with passenger ships. No passengers had been adventurous enough to sign on for this trip, but on later voyages in Eddie's sea year there were often passengers aboard. In this era, it was a cheap way to go cruising to exotic ports if you were flexible as to itinerary and not looking for on board amenities like floor shows or casinos. It was great if you enjoyed reading and you could get into low stakes card games with like-minded travelers.

The view from the bridge and the challenge of navigating a ship over thousands of miles of open water had Eddie wondering if he had made a mistake in choosing engineering over deck. He certainly could envision himself one day rising to the level of Master, but he realized that a twenty or thirty-year career at sea was probably not the future he had in mind. Marine engineering seemed to offer more opportunity to transfer his knowledge and experience to a shore-based occupation. The sea was to be the mistress of his youth. He would settle down to age and grow old with the land.

He had spent the day exploring life topside. Tomorrow he would venture below to really start to figure out what went on in the belly of the beast – the engine room of the African Star.

Dinner that first Saturday night aboard was as Andy had promised – steak and salad night. The steward rang the bell advising that the mess room was open for business at 6 p.m. sharp. Eddie entered and took an open seat at the table. The First and Andy were engrossed in a deep conversation about having avoided the upcoming longshoreman's strike.

Eddie ordered a steak, medium rare, with a baked potato. The steward placed a fresh lettuce and tomato salad in front of him. He was no vegan – a meat and potatoes man all the way as he had been raised in an Irish house. He decided to try this rabbit food because he was hungry. He poured a liberal dose from a bottle labeled "French" dressing on the food, despite being wary of any food with a Gallic moniker. At this time, he thought *filet mignon* was some sort of disgusting French fish – not the queen of all beef steaks.

To his amazement the flavor of the dressing, combined with the crispness of the lettuce and tang of the tomato, was so pleasing to his taste buds that he quickly polished off this appetizer and asked the steward for a second.

Seeing this Andy said, "Careful there cadet, or they'll be no room for ice cream."

The main meal arrived which turned out to be exactly as ordered and delicious – confirming that the African Star was indeed a "Feeder". While all were absorbed in their culinary delight, in walked Rizzo, the Third Assistant Engineer on the 4-8 watch. Dinner time was while he was on duty, but he was relieved by one of the other engineers to eat his meal.

"How's everything below?" asked Leslie.

"No problem First. Everything under control" answered Rizzo.

They conversed about former ships they had served on and people they knew in common. Eddie listened with interest. He learned that the US merchant marine was like a club or network of shared experiences and people. Not unlike the Navy, but without the rigidity and pecking order of rank. If you had the required license you could serve as Third on one ship and First on another and Second on a third.

After Rizzo left, the First turned to Andy as said, "We'll have to keep an eye on that guy".

"Why?" Andy asked.

"I caught of whiff of bourbon on him" replied Leslie, "and it was closer to 12 minutes old than 12 years."

"Oh boy" sighed Andy, "let's hope these reliefs aren't all boozehounds like that last guy."

"Is that like a shorehound?" Eddie asked as a way of joining the conversation.

"Closely related, and some boozehounds become shorehounds as soon as their on board supply runs out."

He explained that Farrell Lines prohibited alcohol in the crew quarters, but most captains did not enforce this with any rigor. A blind eye was turned unless it came to the point that someone couldn't turn to for work.

As Eddie was absorbing this, the steward brought him dessert – the much anticipated ice cream Andy had referred to. He looked at it with some dismay. It was one of those paper wrapped little slabs of vanilla, chocolate and strawberry he remembered from grammar school lunches. Not at all up to the standards of a Feeder. Still he consumed it happily as it topped off an otherwise basic but excellent meal.

After dinner Eddie stepped out onto the deck and was treated to a glorious sunset off the starboard side. As the yellow disc of the sun dipped below the horizon the sky turned from blue to purple, to orange and then red. 'Red sky at night, sailor's delight', he thought. His first day at sea had been a full one. The ship was beginning to feel like a Home, although he wondered what those he left on shore would be doing at this moment.

IN THE BELLY OF THE BEAST

On Sunday after breakfast, Eddie began his tour of the engine room. The First had given him a flashlight and "channel locks", a pair of pliers that was adjustable by sliding one part through a groove or channel in the other, thereby changing the size of nut or pipe one could grip with them. He put the flashlight in the back right pocket of his khakis and the pliers in the left, exactly as every engineer aboard did. Feeling thus prepared, he entered the engine room from the cabin passageway through a watertight door.

All of his senses were immediately assaulted by the sounds, sights, smells and atmosphere of a steam plant on a ship underway at full speed. As he descended the open steel stair treads (called ladders) down to the operating level, he could feel the thermal energy being radiated by the boilers and huge pipes that distributed superheated steam to the main turbines and other equipment. The warm air carried the odors of fuel and lubrication oils and hot insulation. But it was the sound that overpowered all else. A symphony of pitches, from the high alto whine of the turbines to the low rumble of large pumps in the bass section. The background music was of various fluids rushing through ducts and pipes carrying air, steam, oil and water through the veins and arteries of the beast.

In those days, no one wore noise deadening earmuffs. This undoubtedly caused permanent damage to their hearing, but that unfiltered exposure to the sounds of an operating steam plant allowed engineers to acclimate themselves to the ambient noise surrounding them. Most became very proficient in detecting even small changes in the background to the point that they could tell when a small valve or pump had changed position or operating status somewhere in the far reaches of the engine space. They could then easily pinpoint the location of the change and go investigate the cause and fix it if needed, like a maestro hearing a wrong note in the string section of the orchestra and calling out the miscreant violinist for his or her error.

As Eddie stepped onto the operating level he could see the watch engineer Decker engaged in a heated discussion with his oiler. Decker made a motion directing the oiler to leave and appeared agitated and upset. When he saw Eddie, he regained some of his composure and said, "Hi cadet, steer clear of that guy. He's bad news."

Eddie asked why.

"He just called me an MF", the Third said indignantly.

"A what?", Eddie responded.

"An MF – a MOTHER FUCKER", shouted Decker.

Eddie was dumbfounded. He had never heard the expression before and the words shocked him. "Why would he call you that!?", he asked Decker.

"He asked me if I was married. I said no. He then said well how about a girl friend? I said I had none. That's when he said, 'So you must be an MF'", sputtered the engineer.

Eddie could not believe the oiler meant this literally and said, "He must have been joking around."

Decker was having none of it. "Oh he meant it all right, the bastard."

Seeing there was no way to placate him, Eddie decided to change the subject. "So what are these gages for" he asked, pointing to the small control panel next to them.

"Look at the labels" Decker said rather unhelpfully.

Eddie read the words below each one – Main Steam Pressure, Condenser Vacuum, Sea Water Temperature, Shaft RPM, etc. They were indications of the vital signs of the plant and the propulsion turbines that were driving the ship forward. Decker started making notes in a log book on a stand-up desk before the control panel.

"What are you writing", Eddie asked him.

"Recording how that oiler insulted me", he replied.

Eddie could see that the book contained entries on plant parameters. It was meant to be a record of operating conditions of the machinery for use in trending performance or for review in case something later went wrong – a kind of paper "black box" recording. Not really the place for memorializing the charge that he was a suspected MF.

'This guy seems like a real sour man' Eddie thought. That thought triggered a flash memory of his plebe section mate Bob Sauerman whose demeanor was the polar opposite of his name. Bob was a jovial tuba-playing member of the Academy band[7] – an optimist to the core. He was no Decker.

---

[7] Bob often referred to the marching band as the "moving noise" but they were actually quite good.

Eddie's brain often did this kind of free association and went off on tangents until brought back to the task at hand. It was like some kind of internal Alexa who responded to him thinking "sour man" with "Yes Bob Sauerman. He was in your plebe section. He played the tuba. Would you like me to call him?" Eddie consciously refocusing and getting back on track was him saying "Alexa stop". His brain obeyed as would this future digital assistant.

He decided to leave Decker to his bitterness and began exploring the engine room. He noticed there were no chairs anywhere. Those on duty literally "stood watch", constantly on their feet at their control stations or making rounds of the equipment. The licensed engineer was in charge and had additional responsibilities for on-watch maintenance. The 8-12 engineer also was expected to keep the ship's evaporators in good working condition so they could produce pure fresh water for the boilers, drinking, cooking and sanitation. The 12-4 watch took care of lubricating oil purification and supply, and the 4-8 watch had fuel oil and the boilers as their ancillary focus. Thus the three fluids vital to the ship's mission and safety each had its own steward.

The oiler's job (when they weren't hurling gratuitous insults at their nominal boss) was to monitor the equipment, taking readings each hour as they made their rounds. The fireman rounded out the team and stood on the operating platform aft of but within plain view of the main control station and turbines. The fireman made sure that the boilers were producing the steam required at any time. At Full Ahead this meant maximum output, with all oil burners blazing. He also made sure the feedwater pumps were delivering the necessary stream of water to be turned into steam in those hungry boilers.

The fireman was thus a key figure on the watch team. A trip or malfunction of the boiler pumps or equipment at full ahead could result in sudden loss of steam pressure to the main turbines and generators that supplied the ship's electrical power. This sudden "loss of plant" could be disastrous if not quickly recovered as it could leave the ship dependent on a small emergency diesel generator that only provided minimal power for emergency lighting and vital instruments, assuming it came to life as designed. This automatic start signal often proved unreliable.

Without power, the ship would lose steering capability which, in bad weather or in busy waterways, could spell doom. Thus a loss of plant was every watch engineer's nightmare. To a large degree he depended on his fireman to prevent or at least not cause one. The Chief and First Assistant Engineer in turn depended on the watch engineers to keep any equipment malfunction from turning into a dangerous loss of plant – the same untested relief Third Assistant Engineers, one of whom was already a suspected boozehound.

Eddie went down the ladder to the lower level of the engine room. Here the temperature and noise level was much lower than on the operating floor. This was because he now was below the ship's waterline and the seawater on the outside of the hull cooled the entire space and muffled the sound to a degree. There was even condensation on the skin of the ship which was a ¾" steel barrier between Eddie and the ocean on the other side.

He imagined what it would be like if he was down here when a torpedo struck that barrier from a U-boat. Would he even know what struck him or flail in terror to reach the ladder to safety as the explosion ripped a gaping hole in the ship and torrents of the cold Atlantic rushed in to sweep him off his feet? 'Stop' he told his overactive brain as though silencing Alexa once more. Thank God this wasn't a threat cadets had to face in 1961.

This level was where the pumps ruled – dozens of pumps of all types and sizes. Huge motor driven pumps pushing seawater through the enormous condenser which took the steam exhaust from the turbines, turning it back to liquid for recycling to the boilers; smaller pumps supplying lube oil to the massive gears which coupled the high speed turbines to the shaft that turned the ship's propeller; reciprocating steam pumps chugging away to pump water from the bilges below the deck grating, and the high pressure feed pumps that delivered water to the boilers to be boiled and superheated again as steam to drive the turbines.

Eddie walked around this level and entered a small watertight door into a long tunnel which extended over 150 ft. aft of the engine room. This was the shaft alley and was the quietest, coolest part of the ship.

Steamship Shaft Alley

In ships of this design, the engine was near the middle of the vessel while the propeller was of course at the very back of it. In the early days of steam, screw propellers soon replaced paddlewheels because they were more efficient in driving a ship through water. Large ships often had two or three, but most cargo ships had a single screw. In order to transfer the kinetic energy and the 8,500 horsepower of the turbines, which ran at several thousand RPM, to the low speed prop, a set of speed reduction gears coupled the two. But because of the distance between them, a long shaft was required which ran the length of the tunnel Eddie was now in.

Eddie walked along the alley in which the shaft, a steel cylinder with a 30 inch diameter could be seen turning at about 100 RPM. At intervals there were massive bearing housings that supported the shaft and kept it aligned through its entire length. As he reached the end Eddie could see the place where the shaft finally exited the ship. This was the business end of things. Just on the outside would be the huge three bladed propeller cutting a spiral path through the ocean, pushing water behind as it drove the ship forward. A bushing surrounded the shaft as it exited the ship and a trickle of seawater was allowed through to lubricate the shaft as it turned the prop. This was a critical part of the design – too much water coming through could overwhelm the bilge pumps, too little could overheat the shaft and cause it to seize. Either one could require a trip to the dry-dock to fix it. This location was checked once every hour by the oiler to make sure bad things weren't beginning to happen here. To Eddie's untrained eye, all looked good.

He climbed the stairs back to the operating level where Decker was talking with White, who was relieving him and taking over for the 12-4 watch.

"How's everything below Gadget?" asked White who seemed friendly and in a sunny mood compared with the dour Decker.

"Everything's running smooth" Eddie said pleased that his opinion was being sought.

"All right then, go have your lunch. I'll take it from here", as though Eddie and not the other Third was in charge.

Decker seemed peeved by this. "And what would a new cadet know about anything" he grumbled.

"Well the stern tube is well lubed", Eddie said with a confidence he did not really feel.

The two Thirds looked at him, impressed that he had used the proper terminology. "Good, I'll tell the oiler he can skip that on his first round", replied White.

With this small triumph Eddie left the engine room and headed to the mess room for lunch, thinking 'this engineering business is not so hard'.

OPENING A BOOK AND A MIND

After lunch, he decided that he'd learned enough technical stuff for one day. This Sunday afternoon he'd relax. He'd found a folding cot in the closet which would be ideal for sunning himself on the open poop deck at the stern of the ship. He grabbed a book from his Sea Project list and went aft. Eddie was not an avid reader at this stage of his life but maybe he could get into this one which was required reading in any event. Might as well get it over with.

He looked at the cover: *Cry the Beloved Country* by Alan Paton. As Eddie began reading, he learned that it was set in South Africa in 1948 and the main character is a native Zulu minister who must travel from his village home in Natal province to the capital of Johannesburg to help an ill sister. This also will give him a chance to search for his son Absalom who has gone to the capital but has not been heard from since.

Eddie had some difficulty in identifying with these characters. He had had little contact with black people thus far in his life. In his Catholic grade school class there was only a single African American girl, Caroline Bell, who he cannot remember ever speaking with, but then again there were many girl classmates in that category. At St Peter's HS there were no blacks and the only African American plebe at Kings Point was Davy Burkes, a football player that he barely knew. This was more because football players were a cliquish lot who preferred their own company, than because Davy was black. He appeared to be a popular team member but like most of the players, didn't hang out with non-jocks like Eddie.

Oh he did know quite a few black kids from PAL baseball and basketball leagues, guys named Braxton, Sonny or Pee Wee. They were much better athletes than him and he admired them for that. Most lived in the Markham Homes alongside poorer white kids from the "projects". It was just that after the games, they each went their own way and there were no minority families on Pelton Avenue where his family owned a modest home.

Because he played sports with them, Eddie did not fear black teenagers. That role was filled by Puerto Ricans. As American citizens, they had a right to go freely anywhere in the US and after WWII, they began to move into New York City in large numbers. As the newest members of the underclass, they displaced the Irish as that group of former immigrants moved to more upscale areas from their ethnic enclaves in Manhattan's Hell's Kitchen and the South Bronx.

Just like the Irish had done as the new poor kids on the block, the Puerto Ricans formed gangs which often terrorized their new neighborhoods. Although there were few Puerto Ricans on Staten Island, Eddie's fear of them stemmed from reading about them. One horrific incident in particular made an indelible impression. This was the notorious 1956 knife slayings of two white teenagers in a Hell's Kitchen playground by the "Capeman" and "Umbrella Man", names given by the tabloids to members of a Puerto Rican gang. Such violence was unheard of on Staten Island, but Eddie's too active mind could not help envisioning caped and umbrella-wielding Hispanics stabbing him during a pickup basketball game at McDonald's playground near his house. 'Alexa' would remind him of it if he ever thought of Puerto Ricans. What we do not know we fear[8].

As he read *Cry the Beloved Country*, he became more interested in the native people who lived in the country to which he was headed. He had heard the term "apartheid" and knew it signified a society in which mixing of the white and black races was discouraged and in which the whites held the real power, even though a minority.

'Sounds like Mississippi', he thought. He had never visited the deep south but knew blacks there were marginalized and discriminated against, unlike Staten Island where they were merely ignored and absent from his life. He would learn soon enough that there was a big difference between race relations in America and the apartheid system of South Africa. For the moment he put the book aside and dozed off in the sun until he woke sometime in the late afternoon.

Upon returning to his cabin, Eddie heard an announcement on the ship's loudspeaker that the "Slop Sink" was open for business. This was the name of the ship's store which carried snacks and sundry items that could be purchased by the crew. Of particular interest to most of those aboard was cigarettes which could be had for ten cents a pack or a dollar a carton. This rock bottom price was possible because they were outside US territorial waters and Federal and state taxes were excluded.

---

[8]At least one Brooklyn Jewish teen apparently had the same reaction to these murders. In 1998 Paul Simon wrote and directed the "Capeman" a musical about the gang slayings, but it failed to gain a wide audience and the show soon closed.

Eddie had taken up smoking as a high school senior and now had a pack and a half a day habit. He knew it was bad for him and had resolved to quit during this trip, but when he heard the cost of a carton of Marlboros which were normally three bucks, he thought 'I'd be a fool to give up smoking at these prices.'

'Who could pass up savings like that', he rationalized, as only a young man who presumed himself immortal could. So he proceeded to buy three cartons along with some cans of Planters peanuts and candy bars to tide him over between meals.

He had no hesitation in making this investment as he had been told that cadets would be paid $111/month while on ship. This was a princely sum to Eddie as his allowance during plebe year was $8 which his parents sent in an envelope each week. His spending power had increased almost four-fold overnight. This money would finance his future excursions in the ports of South Africa.

SOUTHBOUND ON THE BROAD ATLANTIC

His first day of work at sea began most inauspiciously. At this time in his life Eddie was a world champion sleeper. As soon as his head hit the pillow at night he was out and would remain in dreamland for ten or more hours if left undisturbed. During plebe year the bugle call of reveille at 6 a.m. usually, but not always, did the trick. His roommate provided backup and would shake Eddie awake if needed.

On board ship day workers and 8-12 watch standers were roused at 7:15 a.m. by the oiler so they would have time for breakfast before turning to at 8 sharp. On this first Monday the oiler dutifully knocked on the cadet's door and received acknowledgement that the wake-up call had been received. Eddie then promptly fell back asleep.

At about 9:30 he came to, locked at his watch and – panicked! He was late for work and couldn't blame the commute. He bolted out of bed, threw on his work clothes and practically flew down the engine room stairs. In the machine shop he found the First and Jumbo gathering tools before starting on some maintenance job.

"Well Gadget, nice of you to interrupt your rest to join us day workers", he said laying on the sarcasm with a trowel. Jumbo just grinned benignly, enjoying the cadet's discomfort.

"I'm really sorry First, I didn't hear the oiler", Eddie responded, not quite truthfully.

"Your timing is great – you show up just before coffee time. Well make yourself useful. Go put the coffee on."

Eddie retreated up the ladder to the mess room and pondered what to do next. He drank coffee but had never been expected to actually brew it before, but how hard could it be for an engineer in training?

He found the electric coffee maker, removed the lid and basket and filled it with water. Next he found the ground coffee and filled the basket, then plugged it in. A light came on and Eddie thought, 'That was a piece of cake. Maybe a nice cup of coffee will make up for my late start."

Leslie and Andy came into the mess room at precisely ten and began pouring their coffee into big white mugs.

"Christ cadet, can't you even make a pot of coffee!?" the First yelled as Eddie saw that his nice fresh brew was filled with grounds.

"This is what happens when you put too much in the basket."

"I'll make another pot", Eddie stammered.

"No forget it, we don't have time" as the clock was eating up most of their fifteen-minute break time.

"Andy get the strainer. We'll have to make do".

"It'll make a good paint remover" Andy joked.

Eddie took a sip – 'My God that is strong coffee' - and forced himself to finish it by adding half a cup of milk.

"Well Gadget that's two strikes and it's not even ten thirty", Leslie said as they finished their break and rose to return below.

Eddie was mortified but happy to hear him revert to calling him by that nickname rather than "cadet" which he came to understand was Leslie's way of registering his disapproval, much as his own father might call him Edward if unhappy with him.

The three went back below where they found the Chief Engineer dressed in work clothes and waiting with Jumbo. He motioned for them to follow him around one of the boilers.

The Chief pointed up to a wisp of steam escaping from an inspection port that was secured in place by a large nut. He turned to Eddie and began saying something to the cadet. Eddie could see lips moving, but the words were completely inaudible against the noise of the engine room. 'Oh my God, here comes strike three' he thought as though Rommel was throwing him a high inside curve ball.

In a panic, he began nodding as though comprehending, trying to buy time. At this moment Jumbo tapped Eddie on the arm and motioned him to follow.

Jumbo led him to the machine shop and handed him a tool, "Chief, he want one and a quarter impact wrench."

Eddie could have kissed the wiper for getting him out an embarrassing spot and off on the wrong foot with the Chief Engineer by failing to carry out such a simple command.

He brought the tools to the Chief who proceeded to tighten the leaking inspection port on the boiler and stop the steam leak.

§•§ •§• § •§

After his missteps on the first working day at sea, Eddie settled into a routine which soon became familiar: work, eat, relax, study, sleep. By day he helped the First and the other day workers with routine maintenance tasks in the engine room.

At times, they had work to do on deck, tending to the cargo winches or the steering gear which was housed in a compartment at the stern of the ship. Eddie enjoyed these assignments because they were in the open air and only done in good weather. They also gave him an opportunity to interact with the deck crew. The ranking members of this department were the boatswain or "Bosun" and the ship's carpenter, known as "Chips". These petty officers oversaw the rest of the deck crew, comprised of Able Bodied (AB) and Ordinary Seamen (OS). These ratings could have been found on a sailing or whaling ship of old and their duties were similar, involving handing ropes, chipping and painting, standing lookout, etc. They were the true "old salts" of the ship.

After work Eddie often sunned himself while reading or dozing on the aft deck. Evenings were spent working on the Sea Project. Lights out was about 10 pm followed by an uninterrupted and deep sleep of nine hours or more.

§•§ •§• § •§

The ship's progress towards the equator was tracked and posted each day on a chart in the officer's quarters. It showed a steady 350 miles or so made each day as the African Star moved through sunny skies and calm seas towards its initial destination.

EQUATOR

Saturday August 26 dawned early as the sun rose in the east. Nothing unusual about that. However, as the day wore on and the sun rose towards noon, Eddie noticed that it was no longer directly overhead, but was now slightly to the north of the zenith. This was another first for him. Those who remained in Staten Island would never see the sun in the north but now the ship was passing very near the equator and at this time of year the noon sun would be north of them until they neared home again and things returned to their normal and familiar state. Eddie and the sun would then cease their wanderings and return home, at least for a time.

From the daily position chart, Eddie knew that today was the day that the African Star would reach that invisible boundary that divided the globe into northern and southern hemispheres. This would happen in the late afternoon. On naval ships a ritual was followed in which those like Eddie, who were crossing the line for the first time, were subjected to hazing and indignities. Merchant mariners took this more in stride.

At the appointed time, the First invited Eddie to his cabin to have a drink with him and Andy. He popped open a bottle of champagne and offered a glass of the bubbly to each of them.

"A toast to the newest member of the down under club", Leslie said indicating Eddie as the honoree. He would have preferred a cold beer, but Eddie dutifully took a quaff of the champagne which he found a little sour tasting – he was no wine connoisseur.

"You're lucky you're not on a destroyer, or you'd be pelted with garbage and have to kiss some fat guy's stomach", said Andy. This was a reference to the naval initiation ceremony for first time crossers or "pollywogs" to be turned into "shellbacks" by paying homage to King Neptune who was usually played by a rotund boatswain's mate.

"Well I guess I'm lucky to be only forced to drink champagne and not have to kiss Jumbo's stomach" Eddie responded.

Eddie asked them how many times they had crossed the equator.

"Well I've been sailing for Farrell for twenty-five years, so it must be a couple of hundred" said Leslie.

"Not quite as many for me but I plan to stay on this run so I may overtake you one day old man", Andy commented.

"We've done it so many times It's no big deal for us", said the First.

"Just another day at sea, same as the one before, same as the one after", Andy added, "except we get steak and a movie tonight to celebrate the crossing".

That evening they did indeed have the usual Saturday night steak dinner and, as an additional treat, the deck crew had rigged a large canvas which would serve as a movie screen between the cargo posts aft of the midship house.

After dinner Eddie took a chair out onto the promenade deck and joined the officers. On the main deck below the crew members had also assembled for the show.

Just after sundown, the opening credits of the "The Vikings" were projected onto the makeshift screen in Technicolor. Eddie had not seen this film which was a couple of years old but he enjoyed movies with a lot of sword fighting so this promised to be a good one.

Even at this age however, he had a critical eye and expected historical films to be somewhat true to life. The movie had a stellar cast including Kirk Douglas and Ernest Borgnine and it was narrated by none other than Orson Welles. The main Viking character however was played by Tony Curtis (nee Bernard Schwartz) and, as the story unfolded, Eddie had to wonder if real Vikings were also well groomed pretty boys who spoke with a New York accent. More likely they were fierce unwashed men who spoke a primitive Gaelic with a Nordic tinge.

In any case, the movie was a big hit and the lower deck cheered on the unlikely hero as he fought bravely and won the heart of a princess played by Janet Leigh, Curtis's real life wife. Popcorn was available in a brief intermission as the reels were changed on the projector.

As the movie and the night ended, Eddie retired to bed – thinking he had achieved another first in his young life, doing something no one else in his family at home had ever done – crossing into the southern hemisphere. What other firsts and adventures lay ahead he could only imagine.

BENEATH THE SOUTHERN CROSS

At sea Eddie worked during the day from Monday to Friday. For weekends the First had given him the choice of working in exchange for time off when they got to port. For Eddie that seemed like a no-brainer as there was little to do at sea but work or study anyway and he would gladly have extra time to explore ashore when they reached land.

For Saturday and Sunday, he would stand watch if there was no overtime scheduled for the day workers. This was his first real shipboard interactions with Decker, Rizzo and White who were the responsible watch engineers.

He began one Saturday on the 8-12 morning watch, expecting to find Decker, the assigned Third Engineer in charge when he went below. Instead he found the Second, Andy was standing watch.

"Where's Decker?" Eddie asked.

"Drunk as a skunk" Andy replied. "He couldn't turn to last night so I got the call to take his watch. The Chief confiscated his stash, or at least the bottles he could find that weren't empty. He's in his cabin sleeping it off."

"Wow. I guess he's in trouble now", Eddie said, felling a bit sorry for the Third, who seemed like a pretty unhappy guy.

"Well he'll get docked for the hours lost and written up, but it's just a slap on the wrist. Boozehounds like him just go from one ship to another."

This made an impression on the cadet. As much as Eddie liked a beer, he knew it would not be a good thing if it were freely available onboard. The long days at sea with nothing much to do would be a dangerous time to start drinking. He resolved then and there to never become a boozehound. He would take a drink if offered but he would not keep it in his cabin where it would be all too easy to get into bad habits.

Eddie spent a lot of time while on watch tracing the lines of different systems. This was required for his Sea Project as he had to produce flow diagrams of major systems showing piping, pumps, valves and other components. It also gave him an understanding of how each system worked and also the physical location for operation and control in the engine room.

While engaged in this exercise on the main feedwater system, he noticed that a thermometer on the water line going to the boiler was showing a temperature of 400F. He approached Leslie who was nearby and said, "First, I think this thermometer is broken. It's showing a temperature of 400 degrees.'

"And what's wrong with that Gadget?"

"Well everyone knows that water boils ay 212", incredulous that a First Assistant Engineer wouldn't know such a simple fact.

"Look at your steam tables", said Leslie.

Eddie thought, 'Steam tables? Aren't they what keep the food hot at the Blarney Stone?'

Seeing his blank look Leslie said, "Look up the temperature for water at a pressure of 450 psi."

He went up to his cabin, fished out his marine engineering textbook and sure enough there was an Appendix containing "Steam Tables" which showed that at a pressure of 450 psi, water didn't boil until it reached 440 degrees.

Like St Paul on his way to Damascus, this was a moment of revelation for Eddie – though of a mundane technical fact and not a spiritual awakening. A light bulb flicked on in Eddie's brain. 'Right, the boiling point of water increases with higher pressure.'

This was why cadets were sent to sea after one year of classroom study. There was no substitute for this kind of learning – in an actual steam plant under the tutelage of a seasoned hand like John Leslie. He didn't just give a direct answer to an obvious question. He directed his student to go find the answer himself.

From this time forward Eddie began to understand how the chemical energy of pre-historic forests stored up in the fossil fuel oil was turned into thermal energy in a boiler and transferred to high pressure steam. The steam then was used to create mechanical energy in the ship's turbines which was transferred to the propeller which in turn gave the African Star kinetic energy as it moved through the water towards its destination.

'Sure beats the heck out of the wind', he thought, appreciating how much easier they had it than mariners who sailed this route before the age of steam.

§●§ ●§● § ●§

In the evenings, Eddie continued his Sea Project reading assignment, getting further into *Cry the Beloved Country*. As he read the story unfolded: Kumalo the native minister is welcomed to Johannesburg by Msimangu a local priest and together they begin the search for Absalom, Kumalo's son. He also discovers that his sister Gertrude is now a prostitute and seller of illegal liquor who he persuades to return to their village with her son.

Absalom meanwhile has been arrested for the murder of a white farmer, who was killed during a botched burglary. Kumalo also learned that his son has impregnated a young girl. He persuades Absalom to marry her before the birth and arranges for a lawyer to defend his son.

Reading this, Eddie was struck by its depiction of life in South Africa, at least among the urban black population and he wonders if it is really as sordid as it is described. There are redeeming figures of course in the two native clerics who are determined to restore the values of their tribal village society to the fallen.

With this story still on his mind, at coffee time the next day, Eddie asked his two mentors, "So when we get to South Africa, will it be that different from home?"

"Well Gadget, you'll see what *apartheid* is all about", said Leslie.

"What does it mean?"

"The separation of the races" said Andy. "You won't see whites and blacks in the same stores, restaurants, theaters, cabs. They each have their own."

"And you won't see them mixing, especially men and women. It's illegal to have sex with a black girl. Just remember that", he added.

"Well I wasn't planning to", Eddie laughed.

"The whole system is set up to keep the natives under control. The white Afrikaners are afraid of what might happen if there's an uprising since they're outnumbered ten to one", Leslie explained.

"Just keep to yourself and don't cross any boundaries and you'll be fine. It's a great country – if you're white', Andy said.

Eddie thought the whole idea of a small minority keeping most of the population down was really unfair and un-American, but he decided it wasn't his country so he would follow the advice of his elders and simply abide by the local laws and customs when he did reach port. No political activist was he.

The Chief Engineer continued to virtually ignore Eddie as days went by without a single word passing between them. So it was a shock when

Rommel, seeing him in the passageway outside their cabins, said, "Cadet I saw a diagram of a turbine on your desk. Did you draw that?"

Eddie remembered the picture in question and said, "Yes, I copied it from the turbine manual. But I returned it to your office right after", thinking he was in for a scolding.

"I know you did. I just wanted to say you did a good job on the drawing." With that the Chief went into his cabin.

Eddie thought, 'Well, how about that? The Desert Fox appreciates art, although of a highly technical nature, like a good German admiring a rendering of an artillery piece. What's next?'

§•§ •§• § •§

One day an incident occurred in the engine room that upset Eddie more than he realized. The First spotted a leaking valve near the skin of the ship. It was a small water service valve that needed new packing – a simple job that could have been done easily but the location was difficult to reach. The valve in question was clearly visible but behind a nest of piping that ran horizontally and vertically in front of it. If someone was thin and agile enough, they could climb over and into this cage of piping and work on the leak.

Jumbo was out of the question as was Andy due to their size, so with great difficulty the First climbed up and into what was essentially a cage of small bore pipes. Fortunately, none carried steam or hot fluid so getting burned was not an issue. Once in place, they handed the First the tools he needed and within 20 minutes the job was complete.

Leslie soon realized that getting out was going to be more challenging than getting in. He was now working against, not with, gravity and he needed to climb out, not just slide down as he did getting in. The First was a thin man, but after several minutes of trying to bend his sixty-plus year old knees and elbows into the required position, it became clear that Houdini himself would have been taxed to do it.

The First was becoming increasingly agitated as he struggled and Eddie could sense a rising panic in the older man. Andy and Jumbo also noticed this and tried to calm Leslie down.

"Take a rest First", Andy said.

"A rest! How am I supposed to rest when I can't hardly move?"

"We'll get you out First", Jumbo said trying to reassure him.

He was in no immediate danger but apparently in the tightening grip of a claustrophobic attack. Eddie has heard of this phenomenon happening to men who climbed into tight spaces like a tank or boiler drum through a small access opening. Once inside, they became convinced that the very opening they had entered had shrunk so they were trapped inside with no way out. A pure psychological mirage of course but one that could induce mental terror and possible heart failure if not dealt with.

Eddie could see that the First was hyper-ventilating and on the verge of passing out. "Go get a cup of water", Andy told him. White who was on watch handed him a coffee mug and Eddie sprinted to the water cooler and filled it. He brought it back and passed it to Leslie through the mesh of piping.

The act of drinking and the cool water seemed to arrest the panic and the First began breathing more normally. Meanwhile Jumbo had pried some of the smaller pipes back to give the First more room to bend his knees and they had thrown a rope over a larger pipe above him to allow Leslie to grab onto it to boost himself up. After another quarter of an hour he emerged from his place of confinement.

"Are you okay First?" Eddie asked him, his concern clearly showing on his face.

"I'm fine Gadget, but next time you're going to do a job like that".

"Sure First, I can handle it."

Eddie never knew any of his grandparents who had stayed in Ireland when his parents came to America in 1929, but he began to see in John Leslie what it may have been like to have a grandfather.

§●§ ●§● § ●§

Soon after this episode, there came an opportunity for Eddie to make good on his promise. The oiler on watch had noticed a pipe vibrating in the shaft alley behind one of the bearing pedestals. A loose bracket needed tightening. Not a major problem but if left to vibrate it could eventually cause a leak.

Getting to the bracket was no easy matter. It required someone to squeeze between the rotating shaft and the bulkhead while reaching down with a wrench to tighten the bolts on the bracket. At this time in his life Eddie weighed less than 150 pounds and was lean though by no means muscular. He was however pretty flexible so he just barely managed to twist himself into a pretzel sufficient to reach the target and get the job done.

"Well done Gadget", said the First.

"Now you're in charge of all cubbyhole jobs" Jumbo told him.

"How about me just doing paperwork from now on", Eddie joked.

"Look at him, First, he wants to be Chief already and sit up in the office all day", Jumbo added.

"No Gadget, you need to do the dirty work before you get to push paper. Besides it's more fun", said the First.

LANDFALL

At noon on Wednesday August 30, the ship's position showed them a mere 500 miles from reaching their first port of call at Walvis Bay in Southwest Africa. They should reach land before dinner the next day.

After almost three weeks at sea Eddie was eager to see dry land again, so on Thursday afternoon he began finding excuses to go on deck to look for the first glimpse of the dark continent. In his mind there would be lush jungle foliage hiding exotic life forms even down to the water's edge. He had seen enough Tarzan movies to know what Africa should look like.

So it was something of a shock as he joined a number of crew members along the port side rail as land hove into view. There it was. Africa in all its – sandy glory. He was looking not at trees and vines but desert. If he had consulted the maps in his textbooks, he would have known that Walvis Bay is on the edge of the Namib desert which covers most of Southwest Africa.

Namib Desert Southwest Africa

In 1961 the area was part of South Africa but had formerly been a German colony before WWI[9]. The main economic activity in the region is mining, including diamonds and uranium. Walvis Bay is the main seaport for Southwest Africa and the African Star was offloading equipment and supplies that would be transshipped inland to mining locations.

---

[9] Since 1990 it is now the independent country of Namibia.

Walvis Bay has a good natural harbor, a rarity along this part of the coast which is otherwise unbroken desert right down to the Atlantic. As the ship pulled into the harbor, Eddie could see only a group of low-rise buildings along largely unpaved streets stretching away from the dock. No other ships were in port.

This appeared to be a frontier town clinging to the edge of the continent. No charm about it, but it was dry land and most crew members prepared to go ashore after dinner to see what was afoot there.

The First asked if Eddie wanted to join he and Andy as they too were venturing into town. He readily agreed and the three of them proceeded down the gangway and up the main street. The sidewalks were wooden walkways and they soon came upon a bar with swinging doors just like in a western TV show like Gunsmoke.

They settled in and were soon approached by a well-worn middle-aged waitress – she was no cute dance hall girl or even Miss Kittie.

"Three Castles", said Leslie, ordering a round of the local South African brew. The bottles arrived and as they sipped, Eddie asked if all of South Africa was like this.

"When we get to Capetown you'll see the real thing. This is the boondocks", Andy replied.

"Do they have apartheid here too?" asked Eddie, seeing a black boy about his age stocking bottles behind the bar.

"Yeah but it's a small town so maybe they're more relaxed about it here", said Leslie.

After his third beer Eddie was starting to feel good. He motioned toward the native boy behind the bar and said "I'm going to talk to him".

"Sure, go ahead and make friends", they laughed.

Eddie went over to the bar and said to the boy, "Hi, I'm Eddie. What's your name?"

The native looked uncomfortable but flashed a wide grin and said, "Hi Boss", not responding to the question.

"No I'm not your boss, just an American" Eddie corrected. "Can I buy you a beer?"

"No, no Boss. Me working here" he said, fear rising on his face.

Andy and the First were watching this exchange and burst out laughing.

"Get over here Gadget before you get the poor kid fired by his real boss."

At that moment, in walked the Chief Engineer wearing a suit and tie.

"Hi Chief", said Andy. "Eddie here is trying to make friends with the natives."

Rommel glared at Eddie and said, "Cadet, you're in a different country now and have to obey their laws. Don't think you can change the world."

Eddie was taken aback but said nothing. 'Who's trying to change the world? I was just being nice to a black kid', he thought.

What he didn't yet realize was that in the South Africa of 1961, being nice to the natives *was* trying to change their world.

CAPETOWN

L ate the following day, the African Star departed Walvis Bay and began its two day run to the tip of the continent at the Cape of Good Hope. They hugged the coast and early on Monday the flat-topped Table Mountain appeared above Capetown, their next port of call. As they entered the harbor, Eddie could see this was no Walvis Bay.

Capetown South Africa

Against the stunning backdrop of the mountain, the town spread out with colorful colonial style buildings lining broad streets and squares as far as the eye could see. It was and remains a picturesque city with a very temperate climate, being at the same latitude south as San Diego or Charleston are north of the equator.

The Cape of Good Hope for which the town is named was first rounded by the Portuguese explorer Dias in 1488. But it was the Dutch who first settled here and founded Capetown in 1652. It became a British colony in 1814 and remained so until the Republic of South Africa became an independent state in 1910.

The white population of Capetown and much of the country is a mix of descendants of early Dutch and English settlers. The non-whites, who make up the vast majority, are mainly indigenous Zulu or Bantu tribes with a segment of mixed race people and Asian (mainly Indian) immigrants. Those of Dutch heritage are known as Afrikaners and speak Afrikaans, a derivative of Dutch and German. The British descendants speak English which is the second official language.

Although the country had long been a British colony and had put down a rebellion by the Dutch settlers in winning the Boer War in 1900, both white groups shared power and in 1948 had enacted the *apartheid* laws which essentially codified white supremacy over the majority non-white population. In 1961 it was in full force as Eddie would soon experience.

Unlike Walvis Bay, there were a number of ships in Capetown harbor, including those of the Union Castle Line that served the UK to South Africa route. The first person aboard after they docked was the Farrell Lines port agent who brought the first batch of mail for the crew members. Eddie was thrilled when the Purser handed him several letters. This of course was the first communication he had from home. A letter from his parents conveyed some family news. His brother Jim was back at West Point as a third classman after he spent his summer learning the basics of the military trade at Camp Buckner. This included the fearsome "slide for life" in which cadets had to zip line down from a great height into a lake. Eddie was just as glad Kings Point had no such ritual.

His sister Sheila had graduated from Notre Dame College (of Staten Island, not South Bend) in June and had gone to Europe with some friends. The highlight of the trip was visiting relatives in Ireland. Now she was back and just starting her first real job with the Social Security Administration in New York. His younger brother Dan had just started his freshman year at St, Peter's High School, Eddie's alma mater. So he wasn't the only one embarking on new adventures in the fall of 1961.

The letter was written by his father, but probably dictated by his mother who added her own brief postscript. It made Eddie homesick to see their familiar handwriting and to think of his siblings so far away.

The other letter lifted his spirits as it was one he was relieved to get. He wasn't sure Sophie would take the time to write him as she no doubt was fully occupied with the onset of her own senior year at St. Peter's. But she had and it was full of news and affection. It ended with a reaffirmation of her love and an admonition that he not "think he was a "Travelling Man" like Ricky Nelson, with a girl in every port. Eddie smiled at this reference to a hit song earlier that year. 'Hardly', he thought.

After lunch, The First told Eddie he was free for the rest of the day to explore the first real port of his sea year. He had taken a cash advance from the Purser so had a ready supply of local currency[10] and, equipped

---

[10] Earlier in 1961 South Africa had adopted the Rand as its official currency which replaced the South African Pound. However both were still in circulation which led to some conversion challenges as the Rand was divided into 100 cents while the Pound was made up of 20 shillings and 240 pence.

with a camera like any tourist, he proceeded down to gangway to the dockside where he was approached by a cabbie who offered to show him some of the sights of Capetown for two rand. Eddie knew from the exchange rate that this was about three dollars, so he agreed to the offer.

"Do you like snakes?" the cabbie asked.

"Not really", Eddie replied. Actually he was deathly afraid of them, but fascinated as well. The Staten Island Zoo boasted a world class reptile house that he and his friends often visited as it was within walking distance of his house. As long as the thick glass of their display cases was between him and the venomous creatures he was content to view them.

"I'll take you to the Snake Farm. You can see all kinds there" the cabbie said.

"OK. Why not?" Eddie replied. Might as well see how African snakes compare with those in the Staten Island Zoo.

He got into the taxi which proceeded along a coast road and soon pulled up outside the afore mentioned Snake Farm. He joined a throng of people buying tickets and he forked over a one Rand note and was given a few coins in change.

Eddie entered the farm which had a number of exhibits of native reptiles and their handlers. In one, a genuine Indian snake charmer sat before a cobra with outstretched wings, playing a flute while the snake swayed from side to side. In another, enormous pythons wrapped themselves around natives who appeared unfazed by the possibility that the life could be squeezed out of them in a few minutes if the snake decided to not play nice.

After half an hour Eddie decided he'd seen enough and walked back to the taxi stand where his driver was waiting.

"Now I'll take you to the best scenic view in Africa", he said. As they drove off, a number of those watching the car raised their arms towards them and Eddie waved back as they drove off.

The cab soon began an uphill drive along the scenic road which led to the top of Table Mountain. When they reached it, it levelled out on a perfectly flat rocky surface that stretched as far as the eye could see and the driver pulled over to a parking area on the southern rim of the mountain.

Eddie got out and was treated to a magnificent view of the town below and beyond to the blue waters where the Atlantic and Indian Oceans met. It was spectacular and Eddie asked the driver to snap his picture with that view in the background.

57

View from Table Mountain

As he posed facing the camera, Eddie noticed that the cab had a roof light with the word "Colored" on it. He had not stood in front of the car before so this was his first view of it.

Now he realized that he, as white as any Afrikaner, had been riding around in a vehicle reserved for a different class in the apartheid system. Those good folks at the Snake Farm hadn't been waving goodbye – they had been shaking their white fists at him – a man of their own superior race riding in a colored cab!

Eddie turned to the driver, who himself could almost pass for white, and confronted him saying, "Am I supposed to be in your taxi?", pointing to the roof light.

"Well you are white and entitled to ride in any cab you choose" he replied.

"But whites don't normally take 'Colored' ones, do they?" Eddie pressed.

"No, not the locals, but you Americans are more relaxed about things like that"

"Maybe so, but am I breaking any laws?"

"Well technically, I guess, but no one is going to arrest you."

'Well, gee, that's a relief' Eddie thought, 'I won't spend my first day here in jail'.

Eddie was annoyed that the guy had taken advantage of him and his naiveté and put him in an awkward position. Still he had gotten his money's worth so he merely asked the cabbie to drop him back downtown.

As they approached the town center Eddie slumped down so his lily white (and freckled) face wouldn't be so noticeable in his hired Colored taxi. He told the driver to pull over on a quiet side street where he exited the vehicle without attracting attention.

'How very strange' he thought, 'I'm hiding the fact that I was in the company of a man almost as white as me simply because the powers that be decreed it an offense against their racial prejudices.'

Eddie shrugged at this bizarre policy and began to walk along one of the downtown avenues. Capetown had a colonial feel to it, what he imagined such an important outpost of the British Empire would have been like in its heyday in the last century. The buildings along the street had covered sidewalks and the shops and restaurants had a European atmosphere. It was all quite charming and new to him.

He soon came upon a crowd of blacks who were clustered in front of a store window, each trying to see over the heads of those in front. Eddie saw that it was an appliance store with a television set flickering in the window alongside radios and vacuum cleaners. This being 1961, it was of course black and white and no more than fifteen inches across.

"What's the attraction?" Eddie asked an Englishman who was also looking at them.

"They're fascinated by TV" he said. Seeing Eddie's puzzled look and realizing he was not a local, he explained.

"Television has not yet arrived here, so stores like this are trying to promote it with displays like this."

"No television?" Eddie asked. "Why in the world not?"

"The government is afraid that the telly will corrupt the morals of the population. Even more so they are afraid that the natives will see things like shootings or violence, and get ideas that threaten the peace" he said matter-of-factly.

Eddie shook his head in disbelief. His own family had owned a TV since 1948 and it was now an integral part of American life – news, entertainment, sports – an essential window on the world whose accessibility was taken for granted.

But what the man had told Eddie was true enough. The government controlled all media in South Africa and had decided that state owned radio was all the people needed. They had banned broadcast TV so, although it wasn't illegal to own a set – there was nothing on! (The store had somehow managed to display some canned footage, but there was no broadcast signal in the air.)

It wasn't until 1972 that the authorities relented, partly because of the backlash from the white population who, almost alone in the world, had not been able to watch Neil Armstrong's "one step for man" on live TV in 1969.

They also realized that people could soon receive signals via satellite. So they introduced a state run TV outlet that tightly controlled what was shown. As with everything under apartheid, there were separate channels for the races – often featuring American shows with dubbed in languages. Thus blacks were able to enjoy "The Jeffersons" with George and Weezy speaking perfect Zulu. Whites had their choice of Archie Bunker in English or Afrikaans.

This all was a long way off in 1961 and Eddie just chalked it up to the sheer lunacy that was apartheid. After stopping for a refreshing brew in an English style pub (no games on TV) he hailed a (white) taxi to take him back to the ship.

§●§ ●§● § ●§

At dinner Eddie told the First and Andy about his experience ashore and asked them to explain the rules of apartheid.

"Well the people are assigned to one of four racial categories: White, Colored, Asian and Black. Each has its own facilities that are off limits to anyone outside their race. So you had no business being in that Colored cab", Leslie explained.

"Same with bars, restaurants, shops, movies, beaches – everyone has to go only to their own places" Andy added.

"What makes someone Colored? That cabbie could almost be white."

"Well they are a mix of white and native. The Cape Colored are very light skinned – the descendants of white settlers who messed around with the native girls way back when. He was one of those. But some lighter skinned blacks try to pass themselves as Colored. That's when they give them the pencil test."

"The pencil test?" said Eddie.

"Yeah, if they think someone black is passing off as colored they stick a pencil in their hair and make them shake their head. If it stays in, they must be black as their hair is too curly for it to fall out."

"That's proof of their blood mix?" Eddie exclaimed.

"Yes very scientific isn't it", Leslie said.

"That's how we know the First isn't black" Andy laughed, pointing to Leslie's bald pate.

"So what are the Asians?" Eddie asked.

"Mainly from India. A lot of them have been here for generations and are professional and business owners. Also some Chinese."

"They rank higher than the blacks but can't use white or colored facilities."

NAVIGATORS DEN

A fter dinner, Eddie decided to see what kind of nightlife Capetown had to offer. He dressed in his best civvies – slacks and jacket and tie – and put a few rand notes into his wallet. He walked down the gangway and caught up with the Second Electrician who had debarked just ahead of him.

"Where are you bound cadet?" the electrician asked.

"Not sure. Just looking to see what's going on in town", Eddie replied.

"If you want to join me, I'm headed for the Navigator's Den".

"Sure why not". Eddie was intrigued by the name.

The Navigators Den Capetown

They hailed a cab which soon took them to a club of that name. Eddie offered his share of the fare which was readily accepted. As they entered the dimly lit bar, Eddie could see it was full of men, some of whom he recognized as crew members of the African Star.

"Hi Sparky", one of them said to the electrician. "I see you've got our gadget with you."

"Yeah, I thought he needed to have a guide."

They sat down at the table and ordered a couple of beers. Eddie's eyes adjusted to the light and he could see there was a bandstand and lots of women present, no doubt most of them hookers as this was a seaman's hangout.

Two girls with beehive hairdos approached the table. They were actually attractive in a cheap sort of way.

"Can we join you?" one asked. The electrician said to pull up a chair which they promptly did.

"What's your ship?" the one with the dark hair, asked Eddie.

"The African Star. I'm the engine cadet" he replied.

"Oh see those guys over there? They're cadets too" she answered pointing to a table with some British sailors. She then went over to them and pointed in his direction.

One of them came over and said in what Eddie took to be a Cockney accent "Hi mate. Care to join us for a drink?"

"Sure" Eddie said and excused himself to his fellow crewmen and sat with the four Brits at their table.

"So you're a cadet Yank?" one asked. "So are we, here on the Carnavon Castle". As they exchanged introductions, Eddie discovered their names were Keith, Nigel and two Henrys.

'How very English' he thought, dubbing them Henry I and Henry II.

Eddie soon learned that they were two deck and two engine cadets on a Union Castle passenger ship operating between Southampton and South Africa. Unlike him, they were company cadets hired directly by the shipping line and serving a three-year apprenticeship before becoming ship's officers.

Eddie ordered a round of beers after learning that their rate of pay was about half his own.

"First time in Capetown? Well you've found the best club here for the bands and the tarts, if you can afford them", Nigel advised.

"Really? How much do they charge?" Eddie asked, from purely academic interest as he was not looking to hook up with anyone other than Sophie if he ever got that chance.

"Well they don't come right out with a price list, but if you really want it, the cost of drinks, a taxi to their flat and a 'present' in the morning will run you a at least twenty quid" said Keith.

"If you're on a tight budget, Three Way Mary there will give you a roll for a couple of bob" he said pointing to an older woman sitting with some foreign seamen. She looked like she had been around the block a few times and could be the mother of some of the younger girls.

They all laughed as a band appeared and began playing some familiar rock and roll tunes as a number of couples swayed on the dance floor.

"Keith, time to give us a song" Henry II said as he went over to the band leader in between songs. He nodded and motioned for Keith to come up and handed him the mike.

The band them began the opening bars of "The Young Ones" a tune by Cliff Richard that had hit the top of the chart in the UK that summer. Keith sang the song well enough to earn the applause of the other patrons as well as a free round of beers on the house.

"We really can't stand his voice, but it's always good for one free drink" one of the others said. They were obviously regulars in the Den, coming here each time their ship hit Capetown – about every six weeks.

After a few more rounds, Nigel asked Eddie "Would you like to see our ship?"

"Sure I would. I saw it as we entered the harbor"

"Come on then, let's call it a night here and go back to where we can drink on the cheap"

They departed the club and hailed a couple of cabs which took them to the passenger dock area where the Carnavon Castle was tied up.

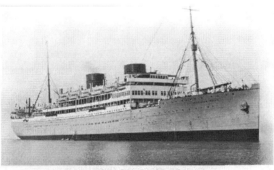

2167. F. G. O. Stuart. UNION CASTLE LINE. MOTOR VESSEL "CARNARVON CASTLE" 20,063 TONS.

The five of them went somewhat nosily up the gangway and entered the wardroom.

On a merchant navy ship, drinks were allowed on board and the wardroom was the center of social life for the ship's officers. Cadets had free access as well and one of them went behind the bar, set five glasses on it and poured liquor from an unmarked bottle into them.

"A toast to the African Star and its foremost cadet", Keith offered as they raised their glasses. Eddie didn't drink hard liquor at all, but he could hardly refrain from doing so now. He raised the glass and took a swig of a cloudy liquid that almost gagged him as it went reluctantly down his throat.

"Your first taste of grog mate?"

"Yeah, what's in it?" Eddie asked.

"A bit a rum mixed with water".

This drink was a tradition on all British naval and merchant ships. Its origin was in days of sailing ships when potable water was in very limited supply. To stretch it out and purify it somewhat, each sailor was allotted a daily ration of rum and water, or "grog" which was considered essential to the health and morale of the ship's company.

In 1961 on a passenger vessel there was of course no shortage of pure fresh water, but British ships are all about tradition, so grog remained a fixture on board them.

After Eddie returned the toast, they asked "Would you like to see our engine room?"

If only to put an end to the grog drinking Eddie said "Of course I would."

The two engine cadets took him in tow and proceeded down into the engine space. The Carnavon Castle was no steamship (SS), she was a motor vessel (MV) meaning her propulsion plant consisted of two very large diesel engines which drove her twin screws while under way.

These huge sixteen cylinder engines stood several stories high and were almost half as long as a football field. As Eddie looked up at these monsters from the operating level, he imagined what a mouse might feel under the hood of a muscle car like a GTO, looking up at its engine.

Since they were in port the main engines were idle but a number of diesel driven generators were running, creating loud background noise over which he struggled to be heard.

"What is the noise like when you're at sea?" he asked.

"You can't hear anything but the engines. We have to use hand signal or notes to communicate" one of the cadets replied.

The smell of diesel oil permeated everything.

While almost all US merchant ships were steamers, Kings Point cadets also learned about diesel plants and would be licensed to serve as engineers on motor ships as well.

As interesting and impressive as this ship's plant was, Eddie decided that steamships were more to his liking. Tending to the steam cycle involved more than just being a glorified diesel engine mechanic. And that pounding noise and the smell of diesel oil? 'Give me turbine whine and bunker C any day' he thought.

After the engine room tour they joined the others in the wardroom.

"Let's go to the cabin. We've got some beer there" said Nigel.

They proceeded down several decks to the crew quarters and entered an inner cabin off a passageway. This was the cadet stateroom. They entered a room about twice the size of his own cabin. As this was home to the four cadets, there was a set of bunk beds on opposite bulkheads. Between them was a built-in table with four chairs. Two small sinks with shaving mirrors were at the foot of the bunks. A door with WC (Water Closet to Brits) on it hid a toilet with no shower. They had to use communal shower facilities down the passageway.

Eddie felt the space was really pretty cramped for four guys but the worst of it was – there was no porthole! As this was a passenger ship, any outside cabin space was reserved for paying customers and lowly crew members like cadets were stowed like cargo inside and below decks. It really made him appreciate his digs aboard the African Star.

One of the Brits broke out a case of Castle beer and Eddie offered to pay for it but they insisted that he was their guest. As they partook of it, Keith took out a guitar and began singing songs some of which Eddie knew and joined in on.

Henry I said to him "Surely a chap named O'Donnell must know some Irish rebel songs".

Being now fully lubricated by all the grog and beer he had consumed, he launched into "The Wild Colonial Boy" a song about Jack Duggan, an Irish Robin Hood who terrorized Australia in the 1800s. He had learned it as a five-year-old and was one of his all-time favorites.

It went over great even though it was about an Irishman robbing and shooting Her Majesty's colonial representatives. Eddie discovered that many young Brits like these really enjoyed Irish rebel tunes, provided the rebels involved are from the nineteenth century and before. They did however frown on those that glorify the IRA who then were domestic terrorists attempting to wrest the six counties of Northern Ireland from British rule.

After several hours, the case of beer was consumed, all known songs were sung and Eddie remembered he had a work day ahead of him. He bade his new found friends goodnight and extended an open invitation for them to visit his ship.

He managed to get down the gangway and began walking unsteadily towards the African Star which was tied up further down the dock. It was now in the wee hours and the ship was quiet except for a local watchman at the top of the gangway. Eddie assured him he was a crew member as he passed by and proceeded to his cabin door.

He fumbled in his pockets for his key which was nowhere to be found! Apparently, he somehow had lost it, maybe when fumbling for pocket change to pay for drinks at the bar.

'What now?' he thought. He couldn't wake anyone one up without causing a scene and getting himself in a lot of hot water.

'The porthole!' He remembered that he had left it open and maybe could get to it from the promenade deck.

Eddie went out on deck and sure enough, it was propped open a few inches and could be pushed back to permit entry to the cabin. It was however not that big – about fifteen inches in diameter and about five feet above the deck.

Resolved to try it, Eddie removed his sport jacket and tie and his shoes which he stuffed through the opening.

'Well I hope this works or I'm going to have a lot of explaining to do when morning comes' he thought.

He jumped up and was able to get his head, arms and shoulders through the porthole. Next he pushed on the bulkhead so that his waist (then a svelte 30 inches) was across the opening. The rest was easy and he soon tumbled into a heap on his cabin floor. Success!

He went over to the door, unlocked it and put it on the hook so the oiler could wake him in the morning, which was now only a few hours off.

Eddie undressed, got into bed and was asleep in an instant.

After what seemed like a minute, he was roused from the deepest alcohol induced sleep he had ever known by the persistent voice of the oiler "Arise and shine cadet, duty calls!"

He rolled over, opened one bleary eye and saw it was 7:15 a.m. sharp. As he sat up, waves of nausea competed with a splitting headache for his brain's attention. 'Fucking grog', he thought, as though the dozen or more beers he had consumed were innocent bystanders in the combined assault on his body.

He had no interest in breakfast, so he managed to use the half hour or so before work to dress himself and go out on deck to get some fresh air. That seemed to help and he shaved and combed his hair. He looked in the mirror and thought 'You don't look half bad all things considered'.

Eddie went below at precisely 8 a.m. and found the First and the watch engineer Rizzo going over some maintenance jobs planned for the morning. Rizzo took one look at Eddie and said with a laugh, "Cadet your eyes look like two pissholes in the snow!"

'So much for my appearing normal' Eddie thought.

Leslie said "Where did you spend the night?"

Eddie told him about his evening at the Navigators Den and the Castle ship.

"Don't hang around with crew members, you're an officer. And English cadets are trouble" he scolded.

"Now we're going to sweat the booze out of you."

Rizzo laughed hysterically at Eddie's discomfit.

"Sure First, it won't happen again" he promised, not sure he really could deliver on it, or wanted to – it had been a fun night even if he was paying the price for it now.

With that, they turned to for the morning's work and Eddie was given some rather dirty and hot work to do in the engine room. This did cause him to sweat profusely which, by noon had him feeling almost normal as he cleaned up and changed clothes for lunch.

'I'm back' he thought as he looked in the mirror and saw the color had returned to his face and his eyes no longer had the forlorn look described by Rizzo. Such was the restorative power of his eighteen-year-old body.

He ate a full lunch which helped him through the afternoon and by 5 p.m. he was fully re-charged. He also approached the Purser to get a new cabin key.

"Leave it ashore at some young lady's bedside?" the Purser asked with a leer.

"No, just mislaid it while drinking with some English guys."

"Oh better be careful around those randy lads" the Purser advised with a wink as he handed Eddie a new key. He promised to safeguard it so he would no longer be required to enter by the porthole.

§•§ •§• § •§

After dinner, although fully recovered from the morning's hangover, Eddie decided that he needed to take a break from partying and to stay aboard for a good night's sleep.

'I guess I'm not ready to join the shorehound club yet" he thought.

He lay down on his bunk as was soon dead to the world.

After some time had passed, something caused him to slowly awaken and he became aware of a nearby presence. He opened his eyes and they met those of a man sitting on his desk chair next to the bunk. With a start Eddie saw – the Purser who was staring at him.

"What – what's going on?" Eddie stammered.

"I saw your door was open and thought you might want some company", the Purser said.

Eddie knew he had left his door ajar on the hook so it was not really open. He caught the whiff of liquor on the Purser. This was really getting weird although he began to suspect the guy wanted more than to keep him company. Eddie got out of the bunk and retreated across the room.

"No, I'm fine. In fact, I'm glad you got me up. I have to work on my Sea Project."

With this the man himself got up and said that in that case he would be going. He stumbled a bit as he left Eddie's cabin.

'What the heck just happened?' Eddie wondered. But he began to figure it out. He knew that some guys preferred other guys like the choirmaster in high school. And when Eddie worked at the local hospital there was a black orderly named Jason who was always hitting on him, calling Eddie a "green-eyed devil". But these were flamboyant types who made no pretense of being straight.

This was something new. The man who had entered his cabin uninvited was a regular guy. 'Christ, I even think he's married' Eddie thought.

Although he didn't know his name – he was simply The Purser- he was an officer and key member of the ship's company. Was he also a homosexual? Did he think Eddie would be open to his advances? Or was it all very innocent?

Eddie realized there were new things he was learning about the people and world around him and that things didn't always appear to be what they were. Without making any final judgements about the man, 'to each their own' he thought, he decided that he best keep his cabin door locked when asleep. Sure the Purser had his own key, but at least he would now know that Eddie's door was not open to any uninvited entries.

Port Elizabeth

O n Wednesday September 6, as the ship neared completion of cargo operations, a sign was posted at the gangway that announced she would be sailing at 6 p.m. This provided notice to crew that anyone not aboard and accounted for would be left behind. To visitors or local workers, it was a remnder that anyone not leaving by the appointed time would be on their way to the next port of call, in this case Port Elizabeth, about 400 miles further along the east coast of Africa.

Eddie observed a group of people being helped aboard with luggage by members of the steward's department. One was a man with dark hair, sideburns and a pencil mustache. He was wearing a string tie and what looked like cowboy boots.

"Who are they?" he asked one of the stewards.

"Passengers. Slim Whitman and his band" he replied.

"Americans?"

"Yeah, he's a country and western singer making a tour of South Africa."

"Never heard of him" Eddie said. And why would he? He was a big fan of rock and roll, and doo-wop music in particular. To him country and western was hillbilly music, not something you heard around Staten Island. 'Why in God's name is a hillbilly singer touring South Africa?' he thought.

Unbeknownst to Eddie, Otis Dewey Whitman, Jr[11] was popular not only in US country music but had a large following in the UK and other British colonies and Ireland where country music shared roots with local traditional music. At this time he was touring South Africa and had booked passage on the African Star which was calling at the same coastal towns and cities where he was performing.

---

[11] Whitman died in 2013 at age 90 and was 38 at the time of this South African tour.

The ship served as both transportation and floating hotel rooms for Whitman and his entourage and provided Farrell Lines with added income and publicity. The band would take her from Capetown to Durban with stops at Port Elizabeth and East London where he had planned appearances.

After all passengers and crew were safely aboard, the ship cast off shortly after 6 p.m. and proceeded to sea for the short journey to Port Elizabeth. On Friday morning before lunch the ship pulled alongside the dock and Eddie could see a small crowd gathered there, a dozen or more and mostly young girls. They were waving at someone up on the deck outside the passenger cabins. Eddie looked up and saw Slim Whitman returning their greeting.

'They're his fans' Eddie thought. He was amazed that an American country singer could attract a crowd (admittedly small) in a place like this. This wasn't Elvis arriving in London on the Queen Mary where hundreds of screaming girls would be dockside. It was a low rent version of the same thing though – a B list singer on a freighter in an out of the way port on the African coast. Impressive in its own right nonetheless.

When the ship was cleared, Whitman and some of his band members went down to sign autographs and remind the fans to attend his performance scheduled for that evening. No doubt he would have a good turnout for it.

After lunch, Eddie went ashore in search of some souvenirs to bring back home. He proceeded up a street from the dock area which soon opened into a central market square. Port Elizabeth was a charming small city with a continental air about it. There was a large square which had a number of stores around its perimeter.

Market Square Port Elizabeth

Eddie could see African art and woodcarvings in the shop windows. He entered one and selected a couple of figurines and masks that were carved of black ebony or lighter tropical woods. They were quite inexpensive which was in keeping with his limited budget.

After purchasing these, he went looking for "tiger's eye" jewelry which his sister Sheila had asked him to bring home. This was an inexpensive but pretty mineral with lustrous bands of brown, orange, black and white – hence the name. It was abundant locally and on display in the shops. With the help of a salegirl he selected a pendant for Sheila and some earrings for Sophie. He hoped they would be pleased and wear his "eye of the tiger" gifts proudly.

Satisfied that he had fulfilled his gift buying duties, he stopped near the square for a rest and to observe the locals. Soon a couple of young girls approached, eyeing him while whispering and giggling. They looked about fifteen or sixteen and were quite cute.

One finally got up the nerve to say "Are you American?"

"Yes, how did you know?" Was it his impressive bearing, an aura of authority and worldliness he exuded that marked him as representative of the superpower that was his country?

"Your shoes. The boys here don't wear those."

Eddie looked down at his penny loafers.

'I guess it wasn't my looks that attracted them after all' he thought ruefully.

After leaving the girls, Eddie decided to take in a movie that he had passed on the way. He returned to the theater which was showing a new Elvis Presley film "Wild in the Country". A matinee showing was starting shortly, so he went in, bought some popcorn and settled in among the few people already seated.

He himself was no big Elvis fan, but the King was very popular throughout the world and his movies were shown in places like Port Elizabeth at almost the same time they were released in the US.

This one, like all his films was mainly a chance to showcase Elvis singing as his acting talents were still a work in progress. Despite that, Eddie settled in and began to enjoy the movie. The plot had Glenn Tyler (Elvis), a troubled young man trying to straighten his life out in a small town while living with an uncle. He dreams of being a writer and – oh by the way – plays guitar and sings!

The movie featured Tuesday Weld and Hope Lange as his love interests, young and older. There were several songs in the soundtrack, including the title song that moved Eddie emotionally as did many other sad ballads. All in all he liked the movie very much even though it made him a bit homesick[12].

On his way back to the ship, Eddie passed a newsstand and bought a copy of Time magazine which was the international edition published weekly and distributed through the world. In South Africa, it was the only source of news from America. He was at the time not much interested in anything but sports and entertainment but thought it would be something to read besides his Sea Project books. He stopped into the Central Hotel bar, ordered a pint of beer and opened the magazine.

The cover and lead story told of the Soviets erecting a wall to separate their zone of occupation from that of the Allies in the former German capital. Without warning the Russians had sealed off their zone and begun constructing the Berlin Wall on August 20 while the African Star was en-route to Walvis Bay. Now it was largely in place and patrolled by Russian soldiers who had orders to shoot anyone trying to cross over into the western zone.

Eddie was outraged by this naked act of tyranny. As a child of the forties and fifties he grew up during the Cold War. He remembered the Korean War and the uprisings by Hungarian and Polish freedom fighters which were brutally crushed by Soviet troops. He was a staunch believer in democracy and the freedoms enjoyed in America, as taught at home and by the nuns and brothers in his Catholic schools.

He read that President Kennedy had strongly condemned the wall as a violation of those concepts. According to Time, conservative members of Congress called for military retaliation while liberals counselled patience and diplomacy. Eddie was confused by this.

'Aren't liberals in favor of liberty?' he wondered.

'And weren't conservatives the ones who were cautious, if not timid, about using military force in its defense?'

The more he read he realized that his dim understanding of these terms had been completely reversed. He was not, nor were his parents and teachers "liberals" – they were in fact "conservatives".

---

[12] Critics thought otherwise. One review in the NY Times described the film as "Nonsense, that's all it is – sheer nonsense – and Mr. Presley, who did appear to be improving in his last picture, is as callow as ever. Elvis has retrogressed."

As for political party affiliations there was no confusion. His family were long time Democrats, like most blue collar immigrants in that era. His dad was also a union man and believed strongly in the rights of labor which was a Democrat base issue.

So of course Eddie's father was a registered – Republican!

However, this was a flag of convenience like those flown by many American ships that registered as foreign for economic or other reasons. At the time Staten Island was represented by one John H Ray[13], a Republican congressman. Ray had appointed Eddie to Kings Point as well as his brother Jim to West Point, so their father thought it wise to align his official political affiliation with that of his congressional representative.

Furthermore, Ray was a member of the House Merchant Marine committee and when Kings Point had threatened to vacate Eddie's appointment because he had not taken the required physical, Ray's office assisted in delaying that action until Eddie had taken and passed the physical exam. Thus a special debt was felt owed to the congressman who after all, enabled both O'Donnell sons to get a free high quality college education, albeit with obligations to serve thereafter.

But their father did not advertise his political apostasy. One who discovered it from voter rolls was Bill Ellsman, the district Democratic leader who one day approached Mr. O'Donnell and demanded answers.

"Tell me this Ed, why in God's name are you a registered Republican?" he asked.

After giving Ellsman the background story Mr. O'Donnell said "I may be a registered Republican but I'll never vote for anyone but a Democrat". Ellsman at once understood and advised that he himself would do the same. Politics, as they say, makes strange bedfellows, at least outside the secrecy of the voting booth.

Eddie read the issue cover to cover, including the sports section that featured the ongoing home run race between Yankee slugger Mickey Mantle and Roger Maris. Mantle had 54 homers to Maris' 58 and the drama involved whether either would break Babe Ruth's record of 60 set in 1927. Many old timers were rooting against these upstarts while the adoring young Yankee fans hoped to see both break the mark. Eddie didn't care one way or the other.

---

[13] John H Ray (1886-1975). Staten Island Congressman 1953-1963.

Eddie had been a diehard Brooklyn Dodger fan through the fifties and so had hated the Yankees during their intra-city rivalry. But his ardor had cooled when Walter O'Malley uprooted his team for Hollywood in 1958 so he no longer followed baseball that closely. He had no dog in the Maris-Mantle hunt but was merely a disinterested spectator. He also could care less about Babe Ruth, another Yankee icon, and his record.

East London

After another day or so of offloading cargo, the ship moved on to its next East African port of East London, less than a day's voyage up the coast. As they pulled along the dock, Eddie could see that East London lacked the charm of Capetown or Port Elizabeth. It was a good deal smaller and its architecture was nondescript.

Unlike the last port, there were no fans gathered to greet Slim Whitman who was to appear in the local movie theater for a concert that evening. Maybe because they feared a small turnout, his manger offered free tickets to all crew members of the African Star – in order to fill some otherwise empty seats.

White, one of the relief Thirds saw Eddie and said, "Hey cadet, want to go see Slim tonight?"

Eddie had no real desire to do so but, as there was not much else on offer, agreed to go along.

So after dinner he and White walked the short distance to the theater. They sat among some other men Eddie recognized as from the ship. As the 8 p.m. show time approached, more people filled in, mostly young folk, some decked out in western garb. By the time the curtain went up there were a couple of hundred in the audience.

On stage were Whitman and four or five band members.

"Yee-haw" he greeted the crowd who returned the favor.

"Just like back in Tennessee", said White with a grin, referring to his home state.

"Definitely not New York" Eddie replied.

The band struck up one of Whitman's hits "Tumbling Tumbleweed" to the accompaniment of a steel guitar and fiddle while he played acoustic guitar. Eddie found himself enjoying the music along with White and the crowd. Whitman had a good voice with a wide range from baritone to falsetto.

Eddie himself was a decent singer and he enjoyed harmonizing with his friends Barry Kiley and John Stacey as they used to sing doo-wop songs on street corners in Staten Island. He and they were good mimics and friends said they sounded just like Dion and the Belmonts on "That's My Desire" which built to a dramatic crescendo ending.

He also was a member of the Kings Point Glee Club during plebe year. He auditioned when he learned that they often went off campus for concerts, some with local women's colleges. It was about the only way to get out before plebes were granted liberty.

Auditioning didn't require much talent – George Rose, the conductor was somewhat desperate for warm bodies. Even Clem Bason, Eddie's future roommate managed to croak his way into the glee club.

Eddie was getting into Slim Whitman's country music and voice, but when he broke into a yodel, Eddie thought "Why ruin a good song with that?" But the crowd loved it – it was Whitman's signature talent – he was a world class yodeler.

His other band members, including a girl with a sweet voice, were featured on a few numbers, but the grand finale was Slim singing his all-time great hit "Rose Marie" which topped the charts in the UK in 1955, and set records for country music there[14]. Eddie and White joined the small crowd in giving him a standing ovation.

After the concert they stopped into a pub for a beer. This was Eddie's first real interaction with White who told him a bit of his own story. He was from a small town in Tennessee. He was 36 and went into the merchant marine late in WWII rather than being drafted. He rose through the ranks and got his Third Engineer's license by age 26. He showed Eddie pictures of a wife and two small kids.

"I miss them a lot, but this job pays well and I take lots of time off to be home with them. That's why I only sail relief jobs."

Eddie began to like this man, who was a devoted family man unlike so many other merchant mariners. White lit a small cigar that he was seldom without. He offered one to the cadet but Eddie declined and instead took out a pack of Players Navy Cut cigarettes and lit up as well.

---

[14] Beatle George Harrison cited Whitman as an early influence.

'Here I am drinking foreign beer, smoking English cigarettes and talking to a southerner in an African bar' he thought, musing on the strangeness of it all.

"If you're from Tennessee, why are you shipping out of New York?" Eddie asked.

"Because that's where the ships are" he laughed. He explained that there were a lot fewer jobs out of closer southern ports like Charleston or Savannah. He did sometimes ship out of New Orleans, but New York by far had the most relief berths of any port.

"What do you think of this apartheid system here? Is it like that back home?" Eddie asked.

"Well I won't kid you, the negroes are not on the same level as whites back home but Tennessee is not Mississippi", white replied.

"We don't keep them off buses or out of restaurants. I attend a Baptist church and we have a lot of colored folks in the congregation. I have no problem with that. Even in the deep south, things are changing."

"This system here is meant to make sure the blacks and other races keep in their place and the whites stay in power forever. That's not right."

The conversation turned to other matters and after another round of beers and smokes, they returned to the ship well before White was on duty for the midnight watch.

DURBAN

After a run further up the coast from East London, on Saturday September 16 the ship entered Durban's harbor and tied up at the docks which were a short cab ride to the downtown area. Because he had heard much to recommend this lovely beachfront city, including Sparky's comment about pretty girls, Eddie lined up with the shorehounds, ready to disembark as soon as the ship was cleared. His plan was to first go to a movie that the Second Engineer had seen in Capetown and highly recommended to him. It was showing at a downtown cinema.

As Eddie walked down the gangway, he began looking for a taxi to take him into town. There was a car there but it already had a passenger, an attractive young woman. He then saw Captain Farnsworth come down the gangway. He was dressed not as usual in his khaki uniform but in what looked like a Brooks Brothers suit with narrow lapels and a skinny tie then in fashion. He clearly was set for some off duty leisure time.

When Eddie turned to greet him, the skipper asked, "Cadet are you headed into town?"

Eddie said he was waiting for a taxi, but Farnsworth said, "You can ride with us" and directed him to the front passenger side of the black sedan. The Captain got in the rear with the woman who kissed him on the cheek.

"Meredith, this is Mr. O'Donnell our engine cadet".

Eddie turned and took the outstretched hand of the pretty, well-groomed girl who was about thirty and dressed in what could be a Dior frock.

"Happy to know you", she said in an English accent.

He returned the greeting.

"Where can we drop you?" asked Farnsworth.

"The Playhouse. I'm going to a movie" Eddie replied.

"Ah right on our way" the captain said as he instructed the driver to the theater.

"Now Ed, if you're going to have a bite or a drink there after the film, make sure you stay on your side of the carpet", he said with a grin.

Eddie had no idea what he meant and said "How will I know which side is mine?"

"Oh you'll know all right", he said mysteriously.

"Stop teasing the poor boy" Meredith admonished. "Just look for some of your shipmates. You'll want to sit with them", she explained.

While Eddie was puzzling over these cryptic instructions, the driver proceeded through heavy afternoon traffic through the heart of the city and then pulled up in front of a large Tudor style building with a broad flight of concrete steps leading up to glass doors opening into a lobby. Eddie thanked them for the lift and the taxi drove off.

The Playhouse Durban

Eddie looked up and saw over the steps a marquee bearing the name "The Playhouse" along with the masks of tragedy and comedy which were familiar symbols of the theater. He climbed the stairs and entered a large lobby with cocktail tables and a bar. There were only a few people there at this early hour. The lobby was bisected by a red carpet leading back to the movie theater. He could see the posters for "The Mouse That Roared". 'Well I'm in the right place', he thought.

He went up to the ticket window and handed in one rand which was the price of admission for the movie that was starting in ten minutes. He entered the theater and found a seat which was easy as there were only a handful of patrons, mostly teenagers or families with young children. Soon the lights went down and a newsreel appeared. Images of burned farms and distraught white families appeared followed by footage showing blacks with machetes and rifles with bandoliers across their chests.

The funereal narrator recounted the terror that the Mau Mau rising had inflicted on the nearby country of Kenya in the mid-fifties. The context for this re-telling was the recent release from prison of Jomo Kenyatta, a native political leader that the white authorities had blamed in part for the rebellion. It had been crushed and the Kenyan government felt it safe to release him as a gesture of reconciliation after seven years of imprisonment as Kenya moved toward independence from Great Britain.

This newsreel was a way for the South African authorities to remind their white populace of the dangers of any loosening of the apartheid laws. As no natives were allowed in the whites only theater, there was no risk of it inflaming them as they would never see it.

This mood presented by this somber message was immediately lifted with the opening scenes of "The Mouse That Roared", an offbeat and funny Peter Sellers comedy. It concerns the small fictitious country of the Grand Duchy of Fenwick that is in dire financial straits. It declares war on the US in the hope that when it of course is defeated, it will receive the same sort of Marshall Plan largesse which rebuilt the Axis powers after WWII, which will save it from ruin. Its mail-armored medieval army of archers crosses the Atlantic on a pig boat and invades New York during a nuclear air raid drill. Long story short, through a series of improbable events, this mouse of a country ends up holding the balance of power between the world's nuclear armed behemoths which it wields to produce peace and prosperity for itself and human civilization in general.

Eddie enjoyed this amusing little fantasy, although he didn't find it the gut busting riot that Andy had. As he exited the theater he saw that the lobby had filled up with many people enjoying a drink and socializing at the end of a day of work or shopping. As he scanned the crowd on either side of the red carpet, he at once understood what the Captain and his girlfriend had been alluding to.

To the right were the respectable citizens of Durban wearing their good finery – ladies enjoying tea, couples having a cocktail, families having a bite on a downtown outing. To the left were what polite society would call the deplorables – hustlers, ladies of dubious virtue and seamen, lots of seamen. Durban was a busy port and the Playhouse was a well-known place to begin your evening with a drink or two or three and maybe hook up with a female companion for a paid or unpaid one-night stand.

Eddie had no trouble seeing where he belonged. He immediately saw Andy and John Wheaton sitting with a couple of girls and he approached their table.

"Hi Gadget. How did you like the movie? Did I steer you wrong?" asked Andy.

"No it was very good" Eddie replied.

"And funny, right?" Andy pressed.

"I laughed like crazy", he fibbed.

"What are you drinking Ed?", Wheaton asked as he summoned a waiter.

"I'll have a beer thanks" Eddie replied.

"And just who is this handsome young man?" said one of the women, eyeing him with interest.

"Girls, this is our engine cadet Mr. O'Donnell" Wheaton answered. "He'll be Chief Engineer before you know it."

"Really? Then we'll have to find him a mate" said the other girl.

They were both attractive, a brunette and a redhead and highly made up. They were in their thirties, much too old for him in Eddie's mind.

'I hope they have someone much younger in mind' he thought.

"Sandy would be his type" said the woman next to Wheaton.

"Yes, I agree perfectly" said the other. Eddie wondered who this Sandy was but said nothing.

After their drinks arrived, the conversation turned to gossip about local doings, music and movies in which Eddie had not much to contribute. After some time, Andy rose and said "Well that's a wrap for me. I have to be back on board for refueling during the night shift."

They bade him good night and Wheaton said, "Why don't we see what's doing at the Edward?"

"Right" said the girls, "There's a good band playing tonight."

"Come along Ed, you may have some fun." Wheaton said to the cadet.

"Sure I have nothing else on", he replied.

"Oh you'll have fun all right if we have anything to say about it" the redhead said suggestively.

Hotel Edward Durban

They boarded a taxi at the front entrance and were soon pulling up in front of the Edward Hotel, an historic landmark building along Durban's beachfront drive. Wheaton paid the driver and the four of them went in and found a table in the hotel's nightclub that was crowded with young people drinking and dancing to a five-piece orchestra.

Eddie ordered another Castle beer. He was acquiring a taste for this local brew that had more body than the Schaefer or Bud that he drank back home. He was also getting used to drinking it at room temperature as they followed the English custom and never iced down the bottles. He was beginning to feel a slight pleasant buzz and enjoying the music when the brunette waved towards a young blond girl who had just entered the club. "Yoo-hoo Sandy, come join us", she called out.

The girl came over and said, "I'm just popping in for a minute."

"Well don't run off, stay for a drink" said the redhead. "This is John Wheaton and this is Mr. O'Donnell. They're officers on the African Star."

"Well I'm just the cadet." Eddie corrected.

"But he'll be Chief Engineer soon" said the brunette.

Sandy looked at Eddie with interest and said "All right I'll join you for a bit".

She pulled up a chair next to the cadet and said "Do you have a first name Mr. O'Donnell?"

"It's Eddie" he answered.

"But you look like a Ricky – Ricky Nelson."

Now this was a major compliment, to be compared with that current pop star and heartthrob to millions of young girls. But it also brought to mind Sophie's reminder to not think he was a "Travelling

Man", that Ricky sang about, with a girl in every port. He quickly pushed that thought from his mind.

"And you look like a Sandra – Sandra Dee" he offered in return and this wasn't just a line. She really did, having short blond hair and a cute face with pouty lips. She also had a good shape that was accentuated by a tight sweater and skirt that hugged her form.

They conversed for a time and Eddie discovered she was twenty-one to his eighteen. He was about to ask what she did when the band leader announced, "And now if we can get our own Sandy Foster to come up and give us a song, the night will be complete".

'So she's a singer. I like that' Eddie thought

"Do you know anything by Sandra Dee", Eddie asked as she got up.

"As a matter of fact I do" she said as she walked toward the bandstand.

The band struck up the opening bars to a song as Sandy began '...When I fall in love, it will be forever...". This was an old standard but one that Sandra Dee had in fact covered and rode to the tops of the charts earlier in 1961. When Sandy was done, the crowd applauded and she returned to the table.

"That was great" Eddie told her, "in fact I think it was better than Sandra Dee's".

She seemed pleased by this and they ordered more drinks to toast her performance. Eddie was now feeling really good and his normal reserve was melting away by the minute. He asked her to dance and they pressed together to a slow tune.

After it was over she said "I have to leave now. Would you mind keeping me company on my ride home?"

He was not about to turn down that offer and the two of them bid the others a good night and climbed into a waiting cab outside the hotel. They sat close together in the rear seat but neither made any further move.

When the taxi pulled up outside her building she said "Would you like to see my flat?"

Eddie of course said he would and he paid the driver. They proceeded up a long flight of stairs to the door of her apartment which was the only one over a store of some sort. She found her key, opened the door and flipped on the lights.

The flat had a small living room with a sofa facing the bedroom which was separated from the living room by French doors that were open. Rather than the couch she sat on the foot of the bed and motioned

Eddie to sit next to her. They began making out and she looked down and picked up his hand.

"What is the ring for?" she asked.

He explained that it was his graduation ring from St Peter's HS. It was a rather cheap ring, with a small aquamarine stone in a 10kt gold setting.

"it's pretty" she said. "Could I keep it until you come back to Durban."

He had told her the ship was heading up to Mozambique but would stop again at Durban in about two weeks on its homeward journey. At this point Eddie probably would have agreed to almost anything so he took off the ring and put it in her hand.

She put it on her finger and held it up to the light, admiring it. She then threw her arms around him and pulled him back on the bed.

'This is it' he thought as he envisioned them both slowly but sensuously disrobing and their passion building to a climax in which he would finally leave behind his virginity as she surrendered to his every caress.

The reality was quite different. As someone who obviously had more experience at this than him, she was the one calling the shots. Before Eddie knew it, their pants were on the floor and she pulled him down on top of her. He had removed his blazer at the start of things but was still wearing his shirt and tie. As they coupled, his shirt got caught in between them and her increasingly frenzied moves resulted in the shirt ripping horizontally but neatly across both front sides just below belt level.

When the deed was done, they both fell exhausted back on the bed. Eddie's feeling of triumphant release quickly gave way to remorse. He had cheated on the one he really loved and – 'Oh my God she has my ring, the very ring I had given Sophie when we went "steady" in high school.' He turned to Sandy who was now breathing softly and contentedly.

"I'd like the ring back" he said without explanation. She sat bolt upright and glared at him.

"So you just used it to get in my pants!" she shouted.

"No, no I gave it to you because I wanted you to have it but I realized I may not get to see you when we come back", he said lamely.

She jumped up, gathered her clothes and ran into the bathroom, slamming the door.

'Now what do I do?' Eddie thought as he tucked his tattered shirt back into his pants.

When she reappeared he said "Look Sandy, you can keep the ring until I get back. It's OK".

"I don't want your fucking ring anymore so I flushed it down the toilet" she said.

"You didn't!" Eddie exclaimed. He rushed into the bathroom and peered into the toilet that was filling up after a recent use. No ring there.

"You didn't do that. You still have it" Eddie said, somehow convinced she was making it up.

Just then the door to the apartment opened and a large red faced man in his late twenties appeared. "What's going on here?" he asked Sandy.

'Oh crap, now I've lost my ring, my shirt is torn and I'm going to get my ass kicked' Eddie thought.

Sandy told the intruder what had happened, but rather than turn Eddie into a pile of mush he said quietly but with just a hint of menace "You'd best be going mate".

Eddie forgot all about the ring, put on his jacket and made a bee line for the door, and down the stairs. This guy was obviously not the third side in an irregular love triangle but Eddie was taking no chances. He flagged down a taxi to get him back to his ship.

After he got to his cabin, he put on his pajamas and now, stone cold sober, reflected on the evening's events. He had lost his ring, cheated on Sophie, his pride and his shirt were in tatters. His first full sexual experience had been more farce than fantastic and not at all what he had envisioned – 'I thought we would be naked, but I didn't even get to take off my tie.'

'Well I still don't have a girl in *every* port' he rationalized in his own defense.

He was full or guilt and embarrassment as he drifted off to sleep but in his last conscious moments he thought- 'but you finally did it.'

THE DAY AFTER

O n Sunday, he rose and had breakfast and decided he needed to atone for the previous night's events. The bulletin board had a list of local churches and services available to the ship's company. He saw there was an 11 a.m. mass at the local Catholic cathedral so he dressed in his tan summer uniform, hired a taxi and got to the church on time. He felt no concern about wearing an American uniform to church in this town on a Sunday morning and he had no clean dress clothes anyway.

Emmanuel Catholic Cathedral Durban

Emmanuel Cathedral was the main church for the Durban diocese. It wasn't at all comparable to St. Patrick's in Manhattan, more like a large parish church back home, but it served the same purpose. Eddie entered and found a seat in one of the middle pews. Soon the choir began and the priests and altar servers entered.

This being 1961, before the Vatican II changes, the mass was in Latin, the altar faced away from the congregation and the participants were all men or boys. These familiar features served to connect Eddie to the mass which would be celebrated in exactly the same way back home later that day. In the few times he attended mass during sea year, whether here, in Japan or India, he took comfort in these familiar rites which were a staple of his life at home.

As he followed along with the Latin prayers, he happened to turn his head toward the choir loft in the back of the church and was amazed and shocked to see – black, Indian and Asian congregants praying along with him! Wasn't this South Africa? Didn't apartheid apply here?

It turned out that, while they were not exempt from the separate facility rules, the authorities turned a blind eye when it came to churches. As long as it was discreetly handled, they would not prevent the races from co-mingling during services.

Eddie felt proud of the Catholic church for embracing all members regardless of their skin color. And he was surprised that there were quite a few native Catholics here in Durban. Where did they come from?

Then he recalled the magazines his parents used to receive throughout the fifties from the Maryknoll society in recognition of the donations they made to the Catholic missionary order. They showed missionary nuns and priests in China and Africa with their flocks of newly baptized Catholics for whom they provided education, medical care and other social services. Perhaps these parishioners in Durban were the result of that missionary effort. In any case they seemed to fit in and were accepted as members of the congregation.

§●§ ●§● § ●§

Having eased his conscience a bit, Eddie decided to go the beach this fine Sunday so he hopped in a cab which dropped him off along the beachfront drive. Durban was known for its beautiful sandy beaches that ran the length of the coastline north of the city. Each race had their own stretch of sand and a sign proclaimed this area reserved for white bathers.

Durban Beach 1961

There were quite a few on the beach, mainly families and young people sunbathing and frolicking in the surf. Eddie had not brought a bathing suit but there were bathhouses which provided trunks and towels so he entered one and changed, leaving his clothes in a locker.

90

He laid his towel out to mark his spot near the water and dove into the surf. The water was warm but bracing as he rode the waves which were a nice size for body surfing. Eddie couldn't believe how nice the sand and water were. But what he didn't know was that these waters just off the east African coast were shark infested. In order to protect bathers from being attacked, shark nets were in place offshore to keep the predators at bay. The beaches on Staten Island were sorry affairs – with gritty brown sand, no waves to speak of and polluted besides. The upside was that no self-respecting shark would ever venture near them.

After a while, Eddie decided his Irish skin had had enough sun so he showered and dressed. He was hungry and thirsty for a cold beer but, this being Sunday, the bars and pubs were all closed. Durban like all of South Africa was a dry town on the Sabbath. However, hotel guests and club members could get a drink on their private premises. Eddie took out a card he had gotten for the local Merchant Navy Club which was open to officers of ships in port.

He directed a taxi driver to the address and soon pulled up outside a building flying the red ensign of the British Merchant Navy. He entered and showed his US merchant mariners card, then paid a small visitor's fee which entitled him to use the club's facilities while in port.

Eddie then entered the rooms which had the appearance and feel of a gentleman's club in London. A bar lined one wall opposite a large fireplace. A number of comfortable chairs surrounded tables. An inevitable dart board hung on the wall ready for any challenge laid down by one member to another. A separate room appeared to be a library. Nautical pictures and memorabilia adorned the walls.

There were a few men present enjoying a drink or snack on a quiet Sunday afternoon. Eddie seated himself at a small table and was soon approached by a black waiter dressed as a steward would be on a British passenger ship. Eddie ordered a pint and a sandwich which soon appeared.

While enjoying his lunch, an older gentleman approached and said "Mind if I join you, young chap?"

He was wearing a blue blazer with brass buttons and a row of medals pinned to the breast. Eddie of course invited him to sit in his own club – he was an actual member no doubt.

"I'm Jack Crosby, former Merchant Navy captain, and what branch are you?" he asked, eyeing Eddie's uniform.

Eddie explained who and what he was to which the man replied "Ah yes a cadet. I was one myself many moons ago."

After some small talk about ships and ports, Eddie said "If I may ask, what are your medals for?"

"Well that's a long story, but if you have time I'll be glad to tell it".

"Sure I'm not going anywhere" Eddie replied, wondering if he had let himself in for a long boring story.

"Well, they all have to do with my service during the war" he said meaning of course WWII.

He then unspun the most interesting story of one merchant mariner's harrowing and heroic experiences during that war. Crosby had been captain of a British freighter which was attacked by a German U boat off Durban in 1943. After shelling the ship and killing two crew members, the Germans allowed the remaining crew to abandon ship which was then sunk with a torpedo. As was their practice, the captain was taken aboard the sub as a prisoner.

"How did they treat you" Eddie asked.

"Captain Hoffmann was the enemy, but he was also a professional naval officer. I was treated well under the circumstances" he said, referring to the U boat skipper.

"While I was aboard, the sub attacked a convoy on her way home from the patrol. As I was a prisoner, I was locked away so as not to see their tactics but later learned that they had torpedoed a Dutch vessel."

"When the U boat got to Bordeaux, I was handed over to the Wehrmacht and taken to a camp for captured merchant navy men in North Germany."

"My uncle Dan Duffy was also in the Merchant Navy and was torpedoed in the Mediterranean in 1942. He was held prisoner in a German camp in North Africa but was liberated when the Allies retook it in 1943" Eddie said.

"He was lucky. I was held until the end of the war in 1945. Even then it was touch and go. As the western Allies approached our camp, the SS moved several thousand of us east towards the ongoing fighting with the Russians. At one point on the march we were strafed by RAF planes and several prisoners killed.

"Fortunately, we were abandoned by the Germans as they finally fled and our final camp was liberated when the Nazis surrendered in April."

"Wow, that is some story!" Eddie said. "What did you do after the war?"

"Well by then, I was eligible for a pension and decided I had enough adventure at sea for a lifetime. I had no family, so I retired here to South Africa which I always loved."

"I now sit and tell my story to youngsters like yourself. Most don't know that U boats roamed these waters as well as the Atlantic and it's a story that should be told."

"You should write a book."

"I'm no good at writing but maybe someone will put it down in a book for me."

"Yes, maybe one day someone will" Eddie replied.

§•§ •§• § •§

They shared another beer before the captain excused himself to go join some other old timers who were playing cards. Eddie thought about how calm his own life had been and was likely to remain unless another war broke out. Given the current tensions with the Soviets this was a distinct possibility.

For now, he was concerned with more mundane matters like learning the ways of this new world he was now in. He was growing in many ways but still had a long way to go. He paid his modest tab, leaving a generous tip for his server. Outside on the street, he hailed a taxi and soon was back aboard wondering what would come next.

Lorenzo Marques

O n Monday the ship finished offloading its cargo and passengers and departed South Africa for its next port of call at Lorenzo Marques in Mozambique. After a three day run up the coast, the African star pulled into the harbor of the capital of the Portuguese colony.

It's hard to imagine today but in the 15th century the tiny country of Portugal was something of a global superpower. Her intrepid explorers Da Gama, Diaz and others opened up the territories of East Africa and established trading colonies there. Five hundred years later they still held substantial colonies, one of which was Mozambique. The port was named for Lorenzo Marques, one of these early explorers[15].

As they finished work that afternoon, Andy said he and Leslie we're going to shore for dinner at one of the local Portuguese fish restaurants and they asked Eddie if he'd like to join them. They would also show him around the city. He of course agreed.

Soon after 6 p.m they dressed and went ashore. The dock area was bordered by a lovely park with walkways and a bandstand. There were a number of local inhabitants strolling, probably after their afternoon siesta. As they walked through town, he could see that it had an Iberian flavor with Spanish or Portuguese buildings, many with red tiled roofs.

Lorenzo Marques Mozambique

After some time, they came to a restaurant with outdoor tables, one of which they occupied.

---

[15] After the Portuguese left, the city was renamed Maputo in 1976.

"We come here for the prawns which are caught fresh locally and are fantastic" said Andy.

A waiter approached and Andy pointed to the menu and said "We'll have two dozen of your best prawns and a bottle of Douro".

"The Portuguese white wine is good too. You should try it Gadget" Leslie said. But Eddie was no wine drinker so he demurred and ordered a local beer.

After some time, the waiter approached with a platter bearing a dozen enormous prawns. These were technically shrimp but were about the size of medium lobster tails. There was also a bowl of fresh salad greens and fresh baked bread with a delicious aroma.

They each helped themselves to several prawns and dug in. Eddie loved fried shrimp but this was a new experience, eating grilled prawns, and he found them delicious. The two older men showed him how to dip the bread in olive oil which was also a new experience as he normally would eat bread and butter. He was even persuaded to taste the white wine which he found kind of sour so he declined any more in favor of the beer which was rather strong. Among the three of them they managed to finish most of the prawns along with the salad and bread

After this delicious and satisfying meal they took a stroll around town to aid their digestion. Andy then said "Let's stop for a nightcap" but Leslie declined saying "I'll leave you young bucks to that. I'm heading back to the ship."

So they bid him farewell and walked towards the street adjacent to the dock where, as usual, there were a number of bars. They entered one and Eddie was surprised to see it was filled with seamen and women, many of whom were black.

"I guess there's no apartheid here" Eddie said.

"That's right" said Andy. "There's no law against mixing of races here. The Portuguese control most of the wealth and power but they don't impose the separation rules as they do in South Africa. These girls are free to compete with the white hookers."

Andy and Eddie took a seat at the bar and one of the black women came over to them. She took a look at Eddie and said to another woman "Baby, come here look at his eyes."

An attractive young black girl about his age came over and said "where did you get those blue eyes?"

"From my parents" he said "where else?"

In fact, everyone in his family had the same eyes as did most of his cousins and many from county Donegal where his parents were born. Evidently though, to an African native living amongst Portuguese, blue eyes were a real novelty.

"What is your name" the black girl asked.

"Eddie. And what's yours".

"I am Baby. Would you like some company?" she asked.

"I'm fine with Andy here" Eddie joked, pointing to the second.

"Well if you change your mind just let me know."

As she left, an older white woman approached them and said "Maybe you would like a nice white girl."

"That Baby", she sniffed "may give you something more than you want for your money" implying that consorting with her may involve some unwanted health risks.

Apparently this white woman was someone who had passed her prime back in South Africa and had migrated to Lorenzo Marques where the competition from other younger white hookers was not as fierce. She had brought her apartheid attitudes with her though and looked down on the black girls even though they were younger and more attractive. Since neither Andy nor Eddie was really in the market for any of their services, they finished their beers and returned to the ship.

As Eddie thought about the encounter he realized it was an interesting observation of the economics of the prostitution trade along the East African coast. He had taken an economics course and knew something about the laws of supply and demand.

In the seaman's bars the number of ships in port dictated demand and the supply of providers (i.e., hookers) and prices they charged. When a US Navy ship came in, as they sometimes did, prices shot up (much to the annoyance of the merchant mariners who were the steady customers). This was because the supply side was somewhat inelastic (housewives weren't going to suddenly enter the market to compete with the pros).

In South Africa apartheid further restricted supply as non-white girls were forbidden to compete for the mostly white customers. Mozambique however was a true open market and the prices reflected that, being lower than in Capetown, even with the influx of white whores who could no longer compete in the closed market of South Africa.

Another feature of this commerce was that these enterprising females were all independent contractors – there were no middlemen (i.e., pimps or madams) involved taking a piece of the action. And they were providing a much sought after service at a market price. If they didn't all have a heart of gold, they at least didn't seem to be ripping off their customers.

Eddie mused whether he should submit a study of the subject as one of his Sea Project reports: "An Analysis of Supply and Demand in the African Prostitution Markets". Somehow he thought it would not be well received by the straight-laced faculty members back at Kings Point – besides it might require more hands on research than he was prepared to do.

§●§ ●§● § ●§

A couple of days later Eddie looked at the dinner menu posted on the bulletin board and was less than overwhelmed by the choices. He recalled the seafood restaurant they had gone to and decided to go himself and sample the prawns again.

After some wandering about town, he managed to find it and went in and sat down at a table. Soon the waiter approached and handed him a menu. Obviously he was not by himself going to consume more than a few of these monster prawns so he pointed at the menu and said "I'll have *half* a dozen." The waiter clearly didn't speak English but seemed to comprehend his intent. He ordered a beer and waited for his food to arrive.

The waiter soon reappeared with a platter of - a *dozen* prawns. When the waiter placed them before him, Eddie indicated to him that he had only wanted a *half dozen*. To emphasize the point, he held up six fingers pointing to the pawns on the plate. The waiter seemed confused so he again held up six fingers and said "No, no, six, I only wanted six."

Thinking he at last impressed upon the waiter that he had brought twice as many prawns as desired, Eddie began eating as many as he could, expecting that he was at least not going to have to pay for more than six.

As he was savoring the feast he was dumbfounded to see the same waiter again appear with a new plate containing *six more* of these enormous prawns. He now had eighteen before him, about as many as he, Leslie and Andy had consumed in total on the previous occasion.

'What in the world did he think I was going to do with all this food?' he wondered.

Rather than say any more he decided to just eat what he could. He managed to consume six, as originally planned. He paid for the lot which came to 120 escudos (about $4) but tipped on only a third of the bill. He would not make a fuss but was also not going to reward the waiter for his obtuseness and lack of common sense.

§•§ •§• § •§

While in Lorenzo Marques, as in most ports, local natives came aboard offering to do laundry, tailoring etc. at rock bottom prices. Eddie took advantage of this service to have his wash done. In the bundle was the infamous torn shirt from his escapade in Durban. When the laundry was returned, the shirt had been repaired, with the torn parts expertly re-woven together.

When Eddie eventually got home, his mom, seing the shirt, commented on this, asking what had happened to the shirt to sustain such damage. He replied that it had been torn accidently while he was engaged in some rough-housing ashore. Fortunately she did not pursue this line of interrogation any further, merely commenting on the nice repair job someone had done.

The shirt remained with him all of sea year as a momento of Durban and all that had happened there.

BEIRA

The ship's next port of call was also in Mozambique, in an outpost called Beira, the northern most point on the African coast that the African Star would reach before heading back south. Beira was a port with limited facilities for offloading cargo. Ships like the African Star were too large to dock and so had to transfer cargo to lighters while at anchor. This resulted in a backup in harbor traffic with a number of freighters waiting at the outer anchorage before they could move in to the inner harbor to offload their cargo.

So the African Star spent nearly a week at the outer anchorage waiting for a mooring nearer the dock area. This was the most boring part of the trip for Eddie as he couldn't go ashore and there was not much going on in the engine room. The weather was humid and hot with a glaring sun that made it uncomfortable to be on deck.

Captain Farnsworth decided this would be a good time for a lifeboat drill. These were required by the Coast Guard to ensure that the ship's lifeboats were in good working order should they ever be needed to abandon ship. So one afternoon the crew members not on watch were called to their lifeboat stations and the boats were lowered away. A C3 ship like the African Star had only two life boats but they were enough, unlike the Titanic, to handle all of her crew and twelve passengers if they were aboard.

Eddie climbed aboard his assigned boat along with a number of other crewmen. His boat was under the command of John Wheaton the Third Mate. The Chief Engineer was also aboard. It was a motor boat and also was equipped with a portable radio, water and food supplies in tins.

The boat was lowered away and they started its small engine and began moving away from the ship.

'Not a bad setup if we ever have to leave in a hurry' Eddie thought.

The life boat engine however soon conked out and began spewing smoke. They broke out the oars and rowed back to the ship where the boat was winched back onboard. The Chief inspected the lifeboat motor and determined that it needed a new head gasket.

"See if we have a new gasket in the spares, cadet" he ordered Eddie.

A few days later, they moved into the inner harbor and moored at an assigned location for cargo operations. Eddie joined Decker and Rizzo who were on deck, peering out at the town which was visible and accessible by launch which shuttled between the ships at anchor and the dock. It was available to crew members who wished to go ashore.

Decker said "It's a long time since I've been here."

"Is it much different now?" Eddie asked

"How the hell do I know cadet; I haven't been ashore yet" he snapped.

"I just meant from what you can see" Eddie said. He wondered 'What's this guy's problem. He's always in a grumpy mood.'

Rizzo chimed in "Listen, I've been here before too. There's a game preserve not far from town. I'm going there tomorrow. How about joining me?" he said to both of them.

"Not me. Too hot and besides I've seen the same animals in the zoo" Decker replied.

"I'll go" Eddie said, relieved that Decker would not be along to ruin the trip. He was what a later generation would call a "buzzkill".

"Great, I've got White to cover my day shift so we can leave after breakfast."

§•§ •§• § •§

Next day, in mid-morning they boarded the launch that ferried people from ships at anchor to the dock. It was a small vessel with open seating for maybe a dozen passengers. As a budding engineer, Eddie was fascinated by its propulsion plant which consisted of an upright wood-fired boiler feeding a reciprocating steam engine which was chugging away. It was just like the lake craft in the *African Queen,* though instead of Humphrey Bogart, the skipper was a local native and Katherine Hepburn was nowhere to be found.

They picked up additional passengers from Norwegian and British freighters before heading to shore. These ships and his own were busy loading cargo from lighters that stood alongside the vessels. This was slow going, as the bags of coffee, tobacco and other agricultural produce had to be manually stacked on pallets which were then lifted aboard by the ships' winches and then offloaded in the ship's holds.

This laborious and inefficient process kept the ships in port days or weeks longer than would be the case for dockside operations, but Beira's infrastructure did not support this. In time, containerships would disrupt the entire industry and make even conventional ship and port operations obsolete, but this was then a decade or more in the future[16].

When they finally reached the launch pier, Eddie and Rizzo disembarked and made their way to a building advertising "Safari Tours". In front were several Land Rover trucks with open seating beneath a canvas canopy.

They entered and Rizzo said "When's the next tour for Gorongosa". Told it would leave within the hour, Rizzo took out a thick wad of local currency and said "Two tickets".

Eddie tried to pay for his but Rizzo waved him off.

"You're my guest. What, do you think I'm a *scorticatore?*"

Seeing Eddie's confusion, he translated "A cheapskate, a stiff."

Rizzo was a forty-four year old New York Italian of below average height with a rapid-fire speech pattern that was sprinkled with street and ethic slang. He was not a "made man" but otherwise would have been a good casting model for the Joe Pesci role in *Goodfellas* some years in the future.

He had taken a liking to Eddie, much as Tommy DeSimone (Pesci) would take the young non-Italian Henry Hill under his wing in that classic movie. Maybe it was the sight of Eddie's hungover appearance in Capetown that made him think they were kindred spirits. In any case Rizzo was determined that Eddie would not have to open his wallet while in his company.

They soon boarded the truck and took their seats. Other tourists joined them and when the seats were filled, the guide introduced himself and the driver who were both locals.

"Welcome to Beira. We will soon be off to Gorongosa where you will see African wildlife in its natural habitat. Since we are the intruders into their home, please be respectful and obey all my instructions. Otherwise, you may become their dinner."

Rizzo leaned over and whispered "Fucking bullshit. This can't be as dangerous as a walk through Harlem. The *moolinyans* there would kill you quicker than any fucking lion." He then laughed uproariously at his little racist joke.

---

[16] In 1956 Malcom McLean had modified a tanker so it coud load truck boxes aboard, thus creating the first prototype containership. He went on to found Sea-Land Services and disrupt the entire industry.

Gorongosa National Game Preserve Mozambique

After an hour or so they reached the park entrance, were checked through the gate and began the tour. The enormous game preserve covered 1500 square miles of natural habitat consisting of tropical forest, savannahs, streams and water holes and hilly terrain. It was crisscrossed by trails which the Land Rover could traverse with relative ease. It was not your Wild Kingdom or Disney African theme park with the tourists and wildlife separated by impassable barriers. Eddie and his companions would be sharing the same space with the beasts they had come to see.

The first group of animals they saw were some African wildebeests grazing contentedly on vegetation on the open grassland. They were in no danger unless lions or other predators approached and then they could easily outrun them given the head start provided by the distance to the tree line.

After seeing some hippos cooling themselves in the sun in a water hole, they stopped for a picnic lunch provided by the tour. This was pretty basic fare, sandwiches and soft drinks and fruit, but it hit the spot as Eddie and the others had worked up a good appetite.

As this point the guide shouldered a rifle and said "Now we'll visit the king of African beasts."

They proceeded along a trail until, off to the left, they could see a group of lions, consisting of several males, a female and a few cubs. A number of other passengers took out their cameras and began snapping away.

Soon after leaving the lions, they came upon a herd of magnificent Afrrican elephants larger than anything ever seen in an American zoo.

"Holy shit, look at the tusks on him" Rizzo said. "They could rip your balls off if he ever got mad enough to charge us."

"Not a pleasant thought" Eddie observed.

Next they approached a stream at which a family of rhinos were to be seen. One of the women passengers asked if they could get closer as she wanted a better shot with her camera. Probably because she looked like she may be a good tipper, the driver left the trail and edged closer to the group to provide her with a better photo-op.

While she lined up her camera, without warning, the biggest rhino lowered his huge head with its massive horn and began a charge toward the Land Rover. With that, the driver put it in gear and, with wheels spinning furiously, sought to reach the trail before the enraged rhino could ram the truck and spill its occupants.

As the Duke of Wellington said of Waterloo – it was a near run thing. Just before the thundering beast could make contact with them, the driver managed to get on the trail again, and the better traction allowed the Land Rover to accelerate and put some distance between the truck and its two-ton pursuer.

Everyone's adrenalin was pumping at their narrow escape. This type of excitement would be hard to find at Disney's Africa.

"That sonuvabitch could've knocked us over and trampled us to death" Rizzo said with a grin.

'That's what I like about Rizzo – always looking at the bright side' thought Eddie.

The guide was more relaxed about it. "They rarely come at us but we've not lost a passenger yet, thanks to Moishe here" he said, indicating the driver.

The rest of the tour was somewhat anti-climactic and in the late afternoon they arrived back at the tour building in town.

"Let's get a beer gadget" said Rizzo. "I know a place outside town where we can get something to eat and a little entertainment too."

They hopped in a cab and drove a short distance and came upon what looked to Eddie like a native village. It was a cluster of grass huts around a clearing. A native who appeared to be the chief bid them welcome and offered seats for a show that was just starting.

Soon a number of native dancers appeared to the sound of drums. They performed a ritual dance while chanting and waving lighted torches and shaking rattles.

Servers appeared with a choice of beer or wine and platters of grilled meat, rice and local vegetables. The food was surprisingly good and Eddie ate his fill along with drinking a couple of beers out of what looked like a coconut shell. It all had an African jungle, if touristy, flavor about it.

After some time, Rizzo leaned over to Eddie and said "Now for dessert."

Motioning Eddie to follow him, Rizzo led Eddie to the outer part of the village and down a row of huts. A number of native women stood nearby smiling at them. Rizzo went over to one and could be seen handing over some cash.

"It's all taken care of" he said to Eddie. "There's your hut. I'm going in here."

Eddie quickly realized that the village had a red light district and this was it. Not knowing what else to do he entered the hut and waited.

'Well, I'm not paying so it's really not my doing' he rationalized, thinking he might soon be joined by a pretty young native girl like Baby the tart who he had met in Lorenzo Marques.

'Might as well enjoy it' he thought, warming to the idea and feeling the stimulating effects of the beers he had consumed.

After a short time, the curtains at the entrance parted and a woman came in. She quickly shed her loose caftan and stood there all in her natural state.

Outside of Playboy, Eddie had not really seen a fully naked female form before, but this was more like National Geographic.

'Wow' he thought, "she's really plump'.

She was no Baby but (to him) a middle aged woman. She had curves all right, but a lot of them in the wrong places. He quickly lost his mojo and indicated that he would not be joining her in the natural state.

She seemed not to be offended by this and why would she be? He was giving her time off with pay, compliments of Rizzo.

He exited the hut and, in a short time, Rizzo also emerged from his carnal appointment, grinning broadly.

"Well gadget, how did you like it?" he asked.

Not wanting to appear prudish or ungrateful Eddie said "Yeah, it was great. So I guess we should head back now?"

"What's your rush? Let's get some more beer and we can come back for seconds on dessert."

"Thanks Third, but I need to get back to the ship."

"Suit yourself, but I'm staying for a bit"

Eddie thanked him for his generosity all day and found a waiting taxi that dropped him back near the launch pier. As he had just missed a launch, he went into a bar across the street. It was the Zanzibar, one of many such named bars in this part of Africa. He went in and ordered a beer at the bar. It was a nightclub of sorts with garish tropical décor. Soon two men nearby struck up a conversation.

"Are you from the American ship" one asked in a heavy Norse accent.

"Yes the African Star. I'm the engine cadet. My name's Eddie."

"I am Sven and this is Lars. Ve are seamen on the *Storstad* from Norway. We can practice our English with you."

"Well my Norwegian is pretty bad, so I'm glad to help you there."
They began a halting dialogue about ships, ports and places they had been while alternating paying for rounds of drinks.

The two young bearded sailors could have come out of central casting for "Windjammer" the documentary movie about the voyage of the Norwegian full-rigged training ship *Christian Radich*. Eddie had come to love the film's sound track which was often played in the Kings Point mess hall during plebe year.

"Did you ever sail on the Christian Radich?" he asked them.

"No that is for the rich *guttseillers*" Lars said.

"The what?" Eddie asked.

"Boy sailors, cadets" Sven said. "We are just poor *sjømenn* - ordinary seamen."

"Well I am a cadet, but not rich." Eddie responded. "Do you have a word for a guy who can't wait to get to port and get off the ship? We call them shorehounds."

"Ah yes, Lars here is a *landhund*" Sven said.

"And you are a *fittehund*" Lars shot back.

"Huh?" Eddie said.

"How you would say it...? Yes! A pussy hound" Lars laughed. "Sven is always looking for girls."

After a couple of hours of steady drinking amid this sort of banter, Eddie was really beginning to feel the effects while his two Viking comrades seemed totally unfazed.

Knowing the last launch left at midnight, Eddie kept a close eye on the clock and, with about a half hour to go, indicated it was time for all of them to leave if they wanted to get back aboard that night.

"One more round on us. We must have an aquavit to cap the night" Lars said.

Soon three glasses of a clear liquid were set on the bar.

"*Skøal*" Sven said as he raised his glass in a toast.

Eddie put the glass to his lips, and following their lead, downed the fiery liquid in a single gulp. His eyes watered and he nearly retched as it hit his stomach and released a warmth that spread through his body. He quickly reached for a tumbler of water and chugged it down.

"You must come to Norway and acquire the taste for our national drink" Lars laughed. "But now we must go."

"Let me hit the head first" Eddie said, needing to relieve himself of all the liquid he had consumed.

When he returned from the restroom, Eddie saw that they now barely had time to reach the launch. They left the bar, stumbled across the street and onto the pier just in time. Just in time that is, to see the stern light of the launch receding away.

"Come back. *Kømme tilbake!*" they shouted in two languages, but the boat continued on its way, leaving them stranded until 6 a.m. when service would be resumed.

They could have hired a private launch, but among them they had no money left so they resigned themselves to spending the night at the launch pier which had a number of hard benches which would have to do.

Eddie dozed fitfully while the two Norwegians snored away. During the night the temperature dropped and it became even more uncomfortable as he was dressed for a safari, not a night out in the open.

A little before six they were wakened by the sound of the engine starting on the launch which was now ready for boarding. Before long they were on their way and Eddie bid farewell to his new Scandinavian friends as he climbed the gangway back to the ship.

Above him Eddie could see the First Engineer looking down at him as he came aboard.

"Where have you been?" Leslie asked.

"I was ashore with some Norwegian sailors but we missed the last boat and had to sleep on the dock."

"Norwegians! Never try to keep up with them. They have hollow legs and can drink anyone under the table."

"I guess you're right First. Now I know" Eddie said.

Shaking his head, Leslie said "Gadget, I believe you're becoming a reprobate. And speaking of reprobates, have you seen Rizzo in your travels?"

"I left him earlier in the day. Why?" Eddie replied without revealing where.

"He didn't show up for the night watch so we had to cover for him. Well get some breakfast. At least you got back in time for work."

Eddie went to his cabin and changed into his work clothes. Then he pulled out his dictionary and looked up the unfamiliar term that Leslie had used to describe Rizzo – and himself. He thumbed through the "r's" until he had found it:

reprobate n – an unprincipled or depraved person; a scoundrel or rouge. Then as further context: "Cemeteries were seldom placed on the north side of a church which was reserved for burial of unbaptized children, criminals, suicides and reprobates."

'Wow. A scoundrel, a rouge, fit only to be buried in unconsecrated ground. That seems a bit harsh' he thought, 'Is that what the First thinks I'm becoming?'

Then he read further that the term is "often used humorously or affectionately".

'Well let's hope that's the case.' He thought. He wanted Mr. Leslie's respect and resolved to mend his behavior for the rest of the trip and avoid the company of the likes of Rizzo, whores and Norwegian sailors.

Later that morning the Chief Engineer summoned Eddie to his office.

"Cadet, since we have no spare gasket for the lifeboat motor, I want you to go ashore and see if you can get one" he said, handing Eddie the old gasket that had been taken from the lifeboat.

"There's a marine supply store up the main street. Go there and see what you can get. Here's some money which should cover it."

"Sure Chief. I'll go right after lunch."

Eddie caught the launch which deposited him back at the pier and he proceeded to the store in question. They had no ready-made gasket but he was able to buy some material to make a replacement.

With his chore done, he was happy to be off work and, with some time to spare, Eddie bought a copy of Newsweek from a stand and then stopped at a restaurant with tables along the street and ordered a coke with a plate of nuts.

While thus absorbed, he happened to look up the street and see, walking unsteadily towards him on the sidewalk, none other than Rizzo. He was wearing a straw hat and some kind of African necklace made of shells.

"Third" Eddie called as Rizzo was about to pass by "are you heading back to the ship?"

Rizzo turned and his face lit up seeing the cadet.

"Gadget, you should have stuck around. They're treating me like a chief!" Apparently his largess was buying a lot of favor at the village.

"You should come back with me" Rizzo said.

"No the Chief sent me here to get something for the lifeboat. The First was looking for you too."

"Fuck them. They don't need me in port."

"Well we're sailing in two days on Friday, so make sure you get back before then."

"Yeah, yeah. I've still got money to spend and I've never missed a ship yet. See you later" as he proceeded on his tipsy way.

Eddie finished his snack and took the next launch back to the ship. Once aboard, Eddie gave the First the gasket material and told him of his encounter with Rizzo.

"Rizzo's gone native" Leslie said to Andy who was listening.

"Well if he doesn't come back to civilization by Friday, I'll take his watch and we'll split his pay the rest of the trip" Andy said, almost hoping that would happen.

"We'll see. My guess is he'll run out of money before then, sober up and will reappear."

"Fucking reliefs – they're all alike. Boozehounds and shorehounds." Andy grumbled.

"And *fittehunds*" Eddie added.

"What?" Andy asked.

"Norwegian for pussy hound."

"Yeah, they're that too" Leslie said.

Turning Toward Home

Sure enough, on Friday morning Rizzo came back aboard, looking less like a tribal chief than a man needing to recover from a colossal binge. Eddie felt sorry for him but was glad he had made it back.

The First told the Third to go sleep it off but be ready for to stand watch at 4 p.m. In the late afternoon, the hatches were closed, anchor weighed and the African Star began its return journey. They would revisit the ports of South Africa to take on cargo to be delivered back to the US east coast.

On Thursday September 29 they tied up again in Durban to load bauxite destined to be turned into aluminum for automobiles or other manufactured goods. While there Eddie thought about tracking down Sandy and his ring but realized it was a lost cause. A life lesson learned.

With a hold full of the bulk ore, the ship departed on the morning tide. All went well until they crossed the bar which defined the harbor entrance and dropped the pilot. Eddie, who had been in the engine room assisting maneuvering, came up from below. Just then the ship heeled over to port as a large wave hit the vessel broadside. He was almost knocked off his feet and, as he and the ship righted themselves, they were then tilted to starboard. The ship was rolling about forty degrees each way, the most motion experienced as yet on this voyage.

They were in the midst of a series of "cape rollers", large swells that originated in the waters south of Africa and grew in size as they encountered the continental shelf along the southeast coast. The coastal waters between Durban and East London were notorious for rogue waves that could reach 60 feet in height and sink or damage ships. While these waves were not of that magnitude, they did manhandle the ship and required good skill on the part of the bridge.

After a number of gut-wrenching rolls, the ship was turned into the swells and the rolling became more a manageable pitching motion as the ship rode up and down the waves.

Just as things had settled down, and Eddie was going to his cabin, a shrill alarm sounded in the passageway. This was the engineers alarm and was the signal that help was needed below. The Chief Engineer and Leslie emerged from their cabins just as the lights flickered and went out.

"That fucking Decker – he's losing the plant!" the Chief yelled to the First.

"Come on Gadget, we'll need you below" Leslie said to Eddie.

The three of them, with Andy close behind, started down the ladder in near darkness, their way lit only by some emergency lights that had come on.

"What happened?" the Chief shouted as he shined his flashlight on the face of the watch engineer who seemed stricken with fear.

"The generator tripped" Decker said. "I think it was carryover because the fireman lost sight of the water level while we were rolling."

Apparently the water level in the boilers had gotten high enough for solid water to flow into the turbines driving the electrical generator which provided power throughout the ship, including the engine room. The turbine and generator then tripped off line plunging the ship into darkness and cutting off power to everything.

The danger now was that the feedwater pumps had also shut down, starving the boilers of water which could cause them to burn up, rendering the ship damaged beyond repair and powerless. They would then be at the mercy of currents which could ground the vessel or cause a collision with other ships in the area. The African Star was dead in the water.

"Secure the fuel pump and close the throttle" the Chief instructed the other engineers. This would avoid damage to the boilers and bottle up whatever steam remained to get power restored

Andy moved to shut off the fuel supply and Leslie closed the throttle to the main propulsion turbine. Soon there was an eerie quiet in the engine room. The phone rang and the Chief picked it up.

"We've got a loss of plant skipper" he said to the Captain who had called from the bridge.

"About an hour if we can get the boilers lit again soon" he advised. "You might want to throw out an anchor."

He was advising the bridge that the ship would be without power for an hour or more and that since they were in coastal traffic, it would be best to anchor the ship.

"Cadet, go up and see if we have water in the boilers" he instructed Eddie. "Take your flashlight and shine it through the gage glass. Shout down whether you can see water."

Fortunately, Eddie this time could both hear the Chief Engineer and understand his instructions. He climbed the ladder to the platform between the boilers and found the water gages. He shined his light through them.

"Nothing showing Chief" Eddie shouted down.

"All right come back here."

114

"First, get the steam feed pump going" he said to Leslie.

Without electrical power, they could use the steam driven auxiliary feed pump to get water back into the boilers. Then they would restart the fuel pumps, light the boilers and produce more steam to get the generators back on line to provide electrical power. Then the entire plant could be brought back and the ship's propulsion restored.

"Come below with me" Leslie said to the cadet. They reached the steam feedwater pump and Leslie began opening valves that would allow it to send water to the boilers.

"OK all set on the water end, now we'll put steam on her to warm her up"

Leslie then cracked open the steam supply valve, expecting to hear the hiss of steam entering the pump drive cylinders. Instead – nothing.

"What the hell! Where's the steam?" he cried.

Just then the Chief came down and said "What's the holdup?"

"I don't know Chief, no pressure here".

"Are you sure all valves are lined up?"

"Yes, it should have pressure up to the main supply valve right here."

"Well, it been a while since we used this steam pump but we never had a problem with it before."

Eddie who had been listening intently then said "First, there's a block valve behind the starboard boiler. Maybe it's closed."

The two senior engineers looked at him like he had two heads. "What are you talking about?"

"Well I traced out the lines for this system and remember a shutoff valve in the steam supply behind the boiler"

"Show us!" the Chief said in a skeptical tone.

Eddie led them to where the valve was and pointed to it.

"Crack it open."

Eddie did as told and they could hear the sound of steam passing through.

"I'll be damned – open it all the way!"

They went back to the pump and this time, when Leslie opened the steam inlet valve a rush of steam was heard. Soon the pump was in motion, delivering water to the boilers.

"Go back up and tell us as soon as you see a level" the Chief instructed.

Eddie resumed his place by the water gages and after a while, water could be seen slowly rising in the glass.

"We've got water" he shouted down.

"Relight the boilers" Leslie yelled at Andy who got the steam fuel pumps going while the fireman lit the burner with a torch. Soon both boilers were firing again and steam pressure was rising.

After some time, the Chief got the generator running and closed the main supply breaker. Lights came back on.

The rest was now easy. Main feed pumps and other critical equipment were restarted; steam pressure rose to the point that the main turbine could be put on line. The Chief then moved to telegraph to "Standby Engines".

"Ready to go when you are Captain" Rommel telephoned to the bridge.

"Stand by the telegraph" he said to Eddie.

Soon after the anchor was raised, the engine room telegraph signaled Slow Ahead and Leslie cracked open the throttle.

"Let the cadet take the throttle First" the Chief said to Leslie "I think he earned his stripes today."

Eddie took over control of the throttle valve and felt a surge of pride as he responded to the bell commands which Decker, not he, now recorded in the log book.

'Wow, the Desert Fox just gave me a battlefield promotion' he thought.

After the ship was again at Full Ahead, the watch duties were turned back to Decker with Andy remaining with him until White relieved them at noon.

Eddie joined the Chief and Leslie in the mess room for lunch.

"That valve must have been put in for some work the last time the ship was in dry-dock" the Chief said to Leslie.

"Right. We were both on vacation and the port engineer didn't mention it when we came back."

"How did you know it was there?" the Chief asked Eddie.

"I had to trace all the systems and make drawings for my Sea Project, so I did that instead of just copying the one in the files."

"Well good thing you did. Otherwise we'd still be down there trying to get the plant back.

"I'm going to give you a job. Take each of the system diagrams and if you find something that doesn't match what's in the engine room, mark them up with your corrections. We want them to show what's really down there."

'Oh great' Eddie thought 'I bought myself more work.'

But he was pleased that the Chief Engineer, as well as his First and Second Assistants now treated him with more respect as an engineer than they did the Third Assistant Decker who clearly was not someone to be trusted.

LEAVING CAPETOWN

T he ship arrived back in Capetown on October 6 to load some South African lobster tails before its departure for home. The port agent once again came aboard with letters from Eddie's parents and from Sophie. These caused him some guilt feelings as he had neglected his own letter writing for much of the trip. Since he had little time left now, he went ashore and bought some postcards as well as the latest copy of Time. He retired to the Mayfair bar, ordered up a Castle, lit a smoke and began writing the cards to his folks and girlfriend. The messages were highly condensed and sanitized descriptions of his adventures along the African coast. The trip to Gorongosa, the natural beauties of Durban and Capetown got mention. Not so the waterfront bars and their denizens, and certainly not Sandy. He ended with genuine and heartfelt wishes to be home among them soon.

His writing duties fulfilled, Eddie opened up the copy of Time to see what was going on in the rest of the world. US-Russia tensions were escalating. The Soviets had doubled down on the Berlin Wall in the face of widespread condemnation from the west. More alarmingly, they had detonated nuclear weapons high in the atmosphere. The US had conducted its nuclear bomb tests largely underground since 1955 so such a blatant show of atomic force was seen as a provocation meant to cow the Kennedy administration. It was a foreboding of new challenges ahead for the young President.

On the home front, Roger Maris had in fact broken the Babe's record when he smacked his 61st home run on the last day of the season. Traditionalists were quick to place an asterisk next to this feat as it was done over 162 games, not the 154 Ruth had to hit 60 in 1927.

After going to the post office and mailing his cards, Eddie returned to the ship. He found the First and Andy in the mess room.

"Well that's all three now. I knew it would happen not just when" Leslie said.

Seeing Eddie, Andy said "your friend White didn't show up for his watch, but he's in there now sleeping it off."

Apparently White, who had rarely gone ashore during the trip, had decided to have one last fling in Capetown. With Decker and Rizzo already written up for dereliction of duty, it was now a trifecta – all three relief engineers had gotten drunk and missed work.

Eddie was a bit surprised at White but he had learned that such things occurred with great regularity aboard merchant ships – it was an occupational hazard for men away from home for long stretches and exposed to the temptations ashore in exotic ports.

Once cargo operations were complete, the sailing time was posted. This time if you missed the ship, it would be a long and expensive trip back home. A headcount was conducted as well as a search for stowaways, always a possibility with people ashore desperate to reach the promised land of America.

With all hands (and no more) accounted for, the ship cast off and, while on deck taking one last glimpse of the great Table Mountain, Eddie encountered Jumbo, the lead wiper, who was enjoying a post-dinner cigar.

"So Gadget, how did you like South Africa" he asked.

"I thought it was great, but what keeps you coming back?" Eddie said, wondering why a man of color would want to be in a place where he was regarded as second class.

"I'm treated like a king here. The Coloreds respect me as an American and the women can't get enough of me – or is it my money?" he said with a loud guffaw.

'I'm guessing the money' Eddie thought, eyeing Jumbo's huge bulk.

Here was an insight into the ingenious, though diabolic, design of the apartheid system. By separating and ranking the various racial categories – it was essentially a divide and conquer scheme. The whites were on top, but the Coloreds were accorded higher status than the natives or Asians. Thus, they had an interest in preserving the system and their privileged, though inferior, place in it. Discrimination, like all things in apartheid was relative.

And the Cape Coloreds already had a reason to think themselves superior to the black population. They were, after all, descendants of Europeans as well as natives. Their attitude was one which kept the system going.

"Would you ever want to live in South Africa" Eddie asked.

"Oh no, my wife would never leave Brooklyn" he responded. "Besides there's no place on earth like America."

So at heart, Jumbo was a believer in the promise that all men are created equal. In South Africa, he was just adapting to and taking advantage of a rigged system. Fortunately for him it was one that he could take or leave at will.

'God bless America then" said Eddie as he left Jumbo in a cloud of cigar smoke.

Looking aft, Eddie could still see the Cape of Good Hope in the dying light of the setting sun as the African Star set a northwest course, which would, in about three weeks' time, bring them back home to the land of the free.

NORTHBOUND

The first day out of Capetown, the Captain conducted an inspection of the crew's quarters – the first since arriving in South Africa. Besides checking on the cleanliness of the ship's living spaces, it was an opportunity to discover and confiscate any contraband (drugs, pornography, exotic life forms, etc.) which could cause difficulties with US customs or immigration officials who had to clear the ship in Boston, their first port back home.

Eddie had been below when the inspection was being conducted, but the First approached him and said "Gadget the Captain says your room is a pigsty. Get up there and clean up the mess."

Eddie was surprised as he didn't think his cabin was that untidy, but he had not taken great pains to attend to cleaning duties while the ship was in port and if he wasn't doing it, no one else was. Unlike the other officers, he had no steward cleaning his cabin.

When Eddie focused on it now, he saw that it was quite dirty. Dust bunnies abounded in little colonies along the floors and on the settee. The sink was caked with dried soap, toothpaste and shaving cream. Mold was beginning to sprout in the shower and the toilet – well let's just say it could use professional help.

He was mortified that he had allowed things to reach this point and that Captain Farnsworth was the one to see it all. As a plebe, he had difficulty adjusting to military life and he and his first roommate Bill O'Gorman had attracted unwanted attention because their room often failed inspection. By November they had both accumulated over 100 demerits and seemed well on their way to an early exit from Kings Point.

Then someone decided the two Irish lads were a bad match and moved Eddie into a room with Charlie Greene who was a paragon of neatness. The deck in his room shone like a mirror and he had shoes to match, spit-shined to a museum quality finish. Once Eddie moved in with him, the demerits stopped and he and Bill, now separated for their own good, managed to survive the year and make it to sea year after all.

From the look of his cabin, it was clear that Eddie did not inherit Charlie Greene's passion for acing inspections, but he resolved to clean the mess and reform his ways. Over the next several hours, he scrubbed, mopped, dusted and washed everything in sight. When the Captain re-inspected it passed with flying colors.

"Now keep it that way cadet" Farnsworth said to him.

"Yes sir, I'm sorry it got so bad, but that won't happen again".

As the ship sailed northward towards home, Eddie spent his days in the engine room where he was now an accepted, though junior, member of the engineering team.

One day Leslie approached him and said "Gadget can you run a lathe?"

Like all plebes Eddie had taken a machine shop course in which they learned the basics of operating various machine tools, including the lathe[17]. While he was no whiz at it, he was capable of using a lathe to perform most of its basic functions.

"Sure First, I think so."

"We need to a make a new bushing for a forced draft fan motor" he said showing him a metal cylinder that had been removed from the motor housing. "Here's some stock metal to work with."

It was a matter of taking the solid piece of steel, drilling out a hole and then turning the outside down to the required diameter to fit back in the motor housing.

It was actually a fairly simple operation. The important thing was to machine the inner bore and outer diameter to a very precise tolerance. Too much metal removed would be too loose a fit, too little and it just wouldn't fit into the opening.

Eddie proceeded to make the required machine cuts, taking frequent measurements with a micrometer. When he thought it was as close as he could come, he gave the finished part to Leslie who then tried to insert it into the motor housing.

"No good Gadget, it's too big' Leslie said.

"But I can't take it down any more or it'll be too loose. It's only a fraction of a millimeter out."

"Yeah but it doesn't fit now" the First pointed out.

Eddie had a brainstorm. "How about if we cool it down?"

"What do you mean Gadget?"

"If we put it in the meat freezer for a while maybe it will shrink enough to fit into the housing. Also, maybe we can heat up the housing to expand the opening."

"You know Gadget, you might just be onto something".

---

[17] "Lathe Nomenclature" was a sure fire sleep inducing instructional film plebes were required to watch. Eddie napped straight through it.

With that Eddie took the metal bushing up to the kitchen and asked the cook to put it in the meat locker.

While that was cooling down, he took a brazing torch to where the motor was located and asked Jumbo to start heating the opening where the bushing was to go.

After a half hour or so Eddie retrieved the bushing from the freezer and brought it in an ice bucket to the motor. Jumbo now had the housing heated up and when Eddie tried to insert the now cold bushing it slid in nicely with the tap of a hammer.

The First who was observing this operation said "Well Gadget that's one way to skin a cat. It fits perfectly and it's a job well done."

"You're now Chief Machinist's Mate" Jumbo said.

Eddie felt proud that he had not only used his practical training but was able to apply his knowledge of behavior of metals under different temperatures to solve a simple shipboard engineering problem.

§•§ •§• § •§

By nights Eddie continued work on his Sea Project. He had at last finished "Cry the Beloved Country" and was ready to write his book report on it. Having seen apartheid first hand, he now understood the context in which the story was written.

The book ended with the execution of the native minister Kumalo's son for his involvement in the murder of Jarvis, the white farmer who had been sympathetic to the blacks. Rather than allow this tragedy to deepen the hatred between their races, Kumalo and Jarvis's son find common ground, with the white man building a new village church for Kumalo's congregation. This allows the minister to continue to tend to the spiritual needs of his tribal community.

As Eddie reflected on the meaning of this fictional message in the midst of the reality of apartheid he began to write:

"In South Africa today, injustice and discrimination are enshrined in law. Nothing will change until both sides embrace the message of Kumalo and Jarvis – the way forward is not one of force or violence to right a wrong – but one of love and common understanding. Those hoping for change will continue to cry for their beloved country until leaders on both sides come forth to heal the wounds and dry the tears with this commitment to peaceful reconciliation and forgiveness."

Unbeknownst to Eddie of course, the agent of that seismic change was at that very moment being held in captivity on Robbin Island within sight of Capetown. Not until 1990 would Nelson Mandela be released and lead the way to the end of apartheid and the peaceful transition to power of the black majority people of South Africa.

§•§ •§• § •§

Having finished his book report, Eddie was about to turn in for the night when the engineers' alarm sounded.

'Christ, is Decker losing the plant again?' he thought.

He went out in the passageway just as the First and Andy were going through watertight door to the engine room. Eddie descended behind them amid clouds of acrid black smoke rising from the operating floor. As he got there he could see flames in front of the starboard boiler. The fireman and Decker we're throwing buckets of sand on the fire, but it continued to spread. Eddie could see that the fire was being fed by fuel oil squirting from a line to one of the burners.

There are few things more dangerous than a fire on a ship at sea. If not taken under control quickly it can spread and result in disaster. Oil fires were particularly dangerous. As did all cadets, he had gone through fire training during plebe year and knew that an oil fire could not be put out with water. Sand would work on a small blaze but this was past that stage.

"Andy secure the fuel supply" shouted Leslie.

"Gadget get that fire extinguisher" Leslie said pointing to one nearby as he grabbed another.

Eddie took one of the fire extinguishers near the boiler. This was a foam extinguisher and, as he was trained, he aimed the extinguisher at the base of the fire and then released a stream of foam. The First was doing the same on the other side.

Meanwhile Andy had managed to shut off the oil supply. The foam soon did its job and the fire was put out, leaving a smoldering mess in front of the boiler.

It was all over in a matter of minutes but the adrenaline was pumping and Eddie discharged the contents of the extinguisher before he realized the fire had gone out. Their quick action had kept a relatively minor mishap from escalating into a life- and ship-threatening conflagration.

Apparently the fire started when the fireman failed to secure the oil supply while attempting to change a burner. Bunker C fuel oil is very viscous and hard to ignite when cold and so is heated before reaching the boiler so it will flow easily through the burner and ignite once in the hot furnace. Once the burner was disconnected, the flare back from the boiler ignited the hot fuel oil. The fire then continued to burn and spread until the supply was cut off.

The Chief Engineer, who had also arrived on the scene, rang the bridge and informed the mate that he would need to reduce speed until the boiler could be returned to service. He then proceeded to throttle back on the main turbine to half ahead.

"First, call out the wipers to clean up this mess" he told Leslie.

Soon Jumbo and the other wipers were busily at work with rags, mops and buckets removing the remains of the fire so the burner could be put back in service. No doubt they saw the silver lining in this near disaster, as they would be paid overtime for their efforts.

Eddie was told he needn't remain any longer so he retired to his cabin, now wide awake from the excitement. Soon the First knocked on his door and entered.

"The Chief wants you to stand watch with Decker from now on until we reach New York" he said.

"He and that fireman are incompetent or half in the bag and he's not on speaking terms with the oiler. We'll be rid of them in New York, but can't trust them alone until then. You can keep an eye on things until then and make sure they don't lose the plant or set the ship on fire. From now on you will stand the 8-12 watch."

Eddie was glad of this for two reasons. He could enjoy his afternoons off to relax or work on his Sea Project. More important, it was a vote of confidence from the senior engineers that he was seen as more responsible than a licensed Third Assistant Engineer.

§●§ ●§● § ●§

As the days went by, Eddie began reading another assigned book. This one was entitled "Bread and Wine" and was set in India, a place he would visit later in sea year. The book provided a vivid description of life dominated by the constant threat of hunger amid grinding poverty among the great mass of Indian people in the middle of the twentieth century. He would soon observe these conditions first hand in places like Bombay and Cochin.

The book's title was a symbolic invocation of the sacramental transformation of simple food and drink into life and soul sustaining nourishment. The author had a way of describing hunger and the act of finding food which made the reader totally identify with people whose lives were absorbed with these existential concerns.

The daily quest was to find simple bread and "ghee" a sort of clarified butter. This was the only sustenance available to them – no meat, no vegetables, no sweets.

As Eddie read, he developed a sympathetic craving for bread and butter, to the point that at some meals, he ate nothing else. The mess room steward had become used to Eddie's sometimes odd meal choices. His gastronomic horizons had expanded greatly during the trip. He was now a big fan of salads and of Russian and French dressings. He also had acquired a fondness for rice, which had never appeared on a plate at home in Staten Island.

While he was open to more variety than ever before, when he occasionally found none of the dinner entrees enticing, he sometimes ordered rice with a side of – mashed potatoes, as though he was carb loading for a marathon.

So when he suddenly asked for nothing more than a stack of Wonder bread and a side of butter, it raised no eyebrows.

Once he finished the book, his appetite returned to normal, a good thing because he was approaching 160 pounds with a waist that would make climbing through portholes a very difficult proposition if ever needed again.

§•§ •§• § •§

For the final week or so of the trip Eddie stood watch alongside Decker. At first the Third Engineer resented the presence of the cadet, but soon realized he was a useful addition – one that relieved him of responsibilities he no longer wished to shoulder. Eddie communicated with the oiler and fireman who readily took orders from him. He tended to the evaporators, testing the water output to ensure that it was pure and salt free.

Decker also took advantage of his new backup to sometimes show up well in the bag and quite incapable of standing watch alone.

Eddie did not report such dereliction of duty because he felt sorry for the engineer who seemed like a sad and lonely soul. Besides he was sure the Chief and First knew what was going on, but chose to ignore it with such a short time remaining. They would be rid of Decker and the other relief engineers in a short time.

§•§ •§• § •§

Their first US port of call was to be Boston as the African Star had cargo for unloading there. Then she would return to New York and officially end the voyage. After New York, the ship would embark on a coastwise trip to Philadephia, Baltimore, Charleston and Savannah, before returning to New York to begin a new voyage to South Africa.

This was the common itineray of American ships at the time – a foreign trip followed by a coastwise loop. It was due to US law which prohibited foreign vessels from moving cargo beteen domestic ports.

It provided a protected source of business for US flagged vessels but it had a cost as well. It was an inefficient way to ship goods betwen US cities and often added port time to ships as they had to sometimes offload and re-load the same cargo between ports. It was another opening for containerization to exploit this ineffiency as it soon did. But for now it was an accepted part of a ship's routine and provided an opportunity for a cadet to see more of the USA.

BOSTON

On Friday October 27, the ship entered Boston Harbor, passing Old Ironsides, the historic USS Constitution tied up there. It was a thrill to see American soil once again and Eddie had never been to Boston, in fact had never been much of anywhere in the US outside New York.

The following day was of course his birthday, when he would turn nineteen. He had mentioned this to Leslie as another reason he was excited about reaching port. Maybe he could have a celebratory drink or two.

The First obviously remembered, as that afternoon, he told Eddie "Gadget we're going to treat you to dinner tonight. You're no longer a greenhorn. You're nineteen now and that's a good excuse to go to Durgin Park."

He was referring to a Boston institution, a restaurant that had been serving up man-sized meals in the meat packing district since 1827. It was in the Quincy Market near Faneuil Hall, a short walk from the pier where the African Star was tied up.

Durgin Park Restaurant Boston 1961

At around six, Eddie, Leslie, Andy and John Wheaton disembarked and proceeded to the restaurant. They were seated in the upstairs dining room, a large room with sawdust on the floor, communal tables with red checked tablecloths and antique hanging lamps providing the illumination. It had a wonderful atmosphere befitting a place that had been feeding rich and poor for over a hundred years.

"You've got to get the prime rib Gadget" Andy said. "You won't be hungry again for a week."

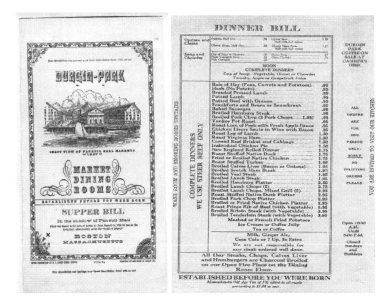

Eddie looked over the menu and saw that Prime Rib was available for $3.95.

'Wow that's a bit pricey, but since they're treating, why not?' he thought.

A waiter appeared and they placed their orders.

"And four Naragansetts "Wheaton said, ordering a round of the local brew.

When the waiter looked quizzically at Eddie, Andy said "Our friend here is celebrating a birthday. Not every day you turn twenty-one" he said, assuring the waiter that Eddie was of legal age in Massachusetts.

Whether the waiter believed this fib or not, he soon delivered four large mugs of beer to the table. Eddie was pleased he had passed for someone two years older.

"Here's to our one and only cadet who's a lot older now than he was a few months ago" Wheaton offered in the way of a birthday toast.

They clinked glasses as they each wished Eddie best of luck. Talk then turned to shipboard gossip.

"Those three bastards are trying to stiff me on overtime" complained Andy referring to Decker, Rizzo and White.

"We had an agreement to split the hours four ways, regardless of who stood the port watches."

Under union contracts, any hours worked at night while in port qualified for extra overtime pay. Andy, as a day worker had the right to work those hours on an equal basis.

Apparently though, as was common practice, the four engineers had agreed they would share equally in this trove of extra money without rearranging schedules. Andy would continue on days but get his share of the money. Now, apparently the three relief engineers were reneging on the deal.

"You'll have to get the union rep involved in New York" Leslie advised him.

Soon the waiter reappeared carrying a tray laden with four platters. Eddie's plate when set before him was overwhelmed by the largest piece of meat he had ever seen. It was a huge cut of pink prime rib with an enormous bone bordering it on one side. It was cooked to perfection with a ridge of fat on the outer side. It was served au jus, i.e. accompanied by a small bowl of beef juice left from the pan.

Along with the beef, there was a basket of cornbread and sides of cole slaw for each of them.

Eddie dug in and soon was quite full even though almost half the meat was still untouched. They ordered more beer to wash down the feast.

When they had all done their utmost to consume these gargantuan slabs of beef, they rested as Andy asked "Still have room for desert Gadget?"

Eddie, though completely stuffed, was never one to say no to dessert so he said "yeah, but give me a minute."

They ordered coffee as they looked over the dessert menu. After a lot of indecision, Eddie chose the apple pie al a mode which was available for thirty-five cents.

At the end of their two-hour repast, the bill arrived and Leslie said to Andy and Wheaton "Eight bucks from each of you and we can cover it and leave a good tip."

Eddie thanked them profusely for the treat. He had never spent as much as six dollars for a meal in his life and was truly appreciative of their generosity.

"Now for part two of the evening" Andy said, "On to the Gaiety."

"I'll be leaving you guys" the First said "my wife wouldn't approve of me going to a girly show. I'll be heading back to the ship."

With that Leslie departed as they made their way to the Gaiety Theater, a short walk from Faneuil Hall.

Gaiety Theater Boston 1961

Eddie had never been to a burlesque show before and was eager to see what it offered – girls stripping down to something very close to their birthday suits.

In 1961, this was the closest one could come to seeing female nudity in public. There was of course no porno and main stream movies or TV were forbidden to show breasts or any other part of a naked female form. A burlesque theater was the best available venue for seeing such things in public.

The Gaiety had a classic marquee which advertised the headline acts and there were pictures in the entrance announcing upcoming stars – strippers with names like Candy Samples and Blaze Starr – not the sort of girls or the names of girls you might bring home.

Andy paid their way in and they found seats among the audience of men with a few brave women mixed in. Soon the music announced the next act and the curtains was raised on a girl decked out in a low cut evening gown with a wrap, gloves and other articles that could be slowly and sensuously removed to the delight and catcalls of the spectators.

Eddie at first found this stimulating as he imagined what was coming as she slowly performed a striptease. The climax of it all was however a disappointment as she ended up not nude, but nearly so, leaving a pair of pasties and a g-string guarding the parts everyone, including Eddie, had paid to see.

But this was Boston and no public display of total feminine nudity was allowed.

Each act followed the same routine and it became monotonous and even ridiculous as some dancers had tassels dangling from their pasties which they managed to twirl, first clockwise and then, to mix it up, counterclockwise.

After an hour or so, they all tired of the routine and decided to call it a night. As they reached the ship Eddie thanked them again for a memorable birthday celebration, unlike any he had spent yet.

On Sunday afternoon Eddie went ashore to catch what was on TV. It had been almost three months since he was able to watch anything, probably the longest stretch of being TV-less since his parents bought their first set in 1948.

He entered a bar near the dock where there were a group of men watching football. He was not a big fan but the idea of being able to sit down with a beer and just watch a game made him feel at home again.

The bar had a black and white TV and it was tuned to the NFL Sunday game which featured the NY Giants vs Dallas Cowboys. He ordered a beer and, this being a waterfront bar, no questions were asked about his age.

At this time Boston or New England had no pro football franchise, but most of the local patrons were clearly anti-NY, probably Red Sox fans who had a visceral dislike for the Yankees which just naturally carried over to the NY football team as well.

As the game unfolded the local fans in the end had a lot to cheer for as the Cowboys edged the Giants 17-16. Quarterback YA Tittle failed to deliver any touchdown passes. The Giants' points were mainly delivered by Pat Summerall who kicked three field goals. This was in the era when such kicking duties were performed by beefy players who could also tackle and block, well before 150 pound soccer players took over that function, after demonstraing they could do it much better.

After the game Eddie went back aboard in time to go below for the 8-12 watch. The ship was due to sail on the evening tide and thus would be maneuvering through his watch. By the time his watch was relieved at midnight, they had cleared the harbor, dropped the pilot and had begun the last leg of the voyage towards home.

Home

After the ship left Boston, it proceeded round Cape Cod towards New York. At one in the afternoon on Monday October 30, the southern shore of Long Island came into view as the African Star neared its final destination.

Eddie went on deck on the starboard side to see if he could spot the first red buoy marking the channel entrance into the harbor. Deck cadets were required to learn by heart the "Rules of the Road" which governed how ships were to be handled in busy waterways – which had the right of way and which must yield in seaborne traffic.

One of the cardinal rules was termed "Red, Right, Returning" which even Eddie knew meant that a ship returning to port had to enter with the red buoys close to its right, well away from outbound traffic which hugged the green markers on the opposite side of the channel.

Eddie found it amusing that deckies used such a simple mnemonic to help them remember such an important and basic rule of navigation. It reminded him of the old joke told about a storied ship captain who each morning would open a safe, take out a piece of paper, read it and relock it away. When he finally retired, one of the crew members summoned up the courage to ask him what was on this mysterious slip. "The secret to my success" the captain said as he handed it to the crewman. On it was written: "Starboard-Right, Port–Left". Some things are just too important to trust to memory.

Soon the red buoys appeared off the starboard side as the ship entered the Narrows separating Brooklyn from Staten Island. It had been eighty days since they last were in this channel with green buoys to starboard as they departed on Eddie's first day aboard. He now felt a thrill of excitement and pride as he reveled in the thought of his homecoming.

The African Star had retraced the path taken by Barthelme Dias and his Portuguese crew as they rounded the Cape of Good Hope for the first time almost five hundred years before. For Eddie, this had also been a voyage of discovery no less profound in his own life. His horizons were no longer those of a parochial school boy and child of the fifties. He had been thrust alone among the company of men, some rough and hardened by lives spent at sea. He had not only survived but cut out his own place and made his mark among them.

Eddie still thought of himself as a boy but he no longer was. By all objective measures he was now a man; a man ready to take on the new decade which lay before him. He could look back upon, but never return to, his days of innocence before this trip.

As he watched the familiar shores of New York harbor glide by, he was reminded of "Home from the Hill" a movie he had seen earlier that year and these words sprang to mind:

> Home is the hunter, home from the hill
> And the sailor home from the sea.[18]

Yes, he the hunter, and he the sailor, was home again.

---

[18] Epitaph of Robert Louis Stevenson

POSTSCRIPT

On Halloween, the voyage officially ended with the African Star tied up in Brooklyn. The crew was paid off and those that were staying aboard signed on for the next trip as well.

A Kings Point rep came aboard to get a report on Eddie's tenure as engine cadet. Reverting to form, the Chief Engineer told him that he was too busy to be bothered. John Leslie however gave him high marks for his performance and behavior (the words reprobate and pigsty were not mentioned). Eddie thanked the First for all his support and mentoring. He truly would miss this fine and gentle man – a proxy grandfather in all but name.

After a few days at home when he reconnected with family, friends and Sophie, Eddie reported aboard his next ship, the US Lines American Flyer bound for Europe. As there were no available deck cadets, he would again sail solo. In the next three months he would make two round trip crossings of the North Atlantic in the dead of winter. The American Flyer was a C2 ship, smaller and slower than the African Star. On the westbound crossings she was battered by storms and wintry gales which caused her to roll and pitch for days on end. To his surprise, Eddie proved a good sailor in bad weather. He got used to the constant motion and never got seasick.

Although he had no cadet companion on the Flyer, there was a young Third Engineer aboard, "Moose" Rehneer who had graduated that July from Kings Point. Eddie knew Moose, who had been a football player and a first classman in his company. As the youngest aboard, they bonded and shared a number of adventures in London, Le Havre and Rotterdam, the ship's main European ports of call.

In April he was assigned to the President Garfield, an American President Lines (APL) ship on a round the world voyage. He finally was paired with a deck cadet, John Murdock who was awaiting assignment in New York as Eddie came off the American Flyer.

This voyage was the Holy Grail of sea year. Everyone hoped for an APL round the world berth. The westbound itinerary took the ship down the east coast, through the Panama Canal, up the west coast to the ship's home port in San Francisco. There she officially began a new voyage across the Pacific to ports in the Far East, then to India and through the Suez Canal to the Mediterranean. From there she passed through the

Straits of Gibraltar before completing her last leg across the Atlantic back to New York.

It was not only the exotic and extensive list of ports that made this a much sought-after assignment for cadets. The President Garfield was a Mariner class vessel, built in 1952 so not yet ten years in service. It was larger, faster and with more amenities than the World War II vintage C class ships. It in fact carried twelve adventurous (if somewhat elderly) passengers who wished to see the world by sea.

After some initial standoffishness, Eddie and Murdock became fast friends as they had a similar sense of humor and outlook on things. They spent most of their time ashore together, exploring places such as Hong Honk, Singapore, Bombay, Athens and Naples. In Genoa they met up with fellow cadets Pete Devlin and Clem Bason, who would be Eddie's roommate for their last two years at Kings Point.

The President Garfield also delivered military supplies to Saigon where the two cadets witnessed the early buildup of US forces in Vietnam, a sobering glimpse of the future.

When they left the ship in May, they chose South America for their last sea year voyage and were assigned to the Santa Elisa, of the Grace Lines. This ship, another C2, took them to Haiti and Panama, then through the canal and down the west coast of South America to ports in Peru, Ecuador and Chile. The return voyage back through the canal ended on July 2, 1962 in New York.

After five voyages to as many continents, and twenty-four countries over seven seas and oceans, Sea Year had come to an end.

§●§ ●§● § ●§

Eddie's life after this momentous year began on a downward note. He discovered that in his absence Sophie had dumped him for a new boyfriend. He returned to Kings Point that fall at the onset of the Cuban missile crisis. His 20th birthday fell on the very day when it appeared that all out nuclear war was imminent. That day, a Sunday, he returned to the campus where an air raid drill was conducted. Perhaps in the basement of Rogers Hall, he and his fellow cadets would survive the Russian bombs dropped on Manhattan fifteen miles away.

These twin crises soon passed. Khrushchev backed down before a resolute President Kennedy - Eddie would live to see twenty-one after all. Sophie soon reappeared in his life, asking to be taken back after her new love interest proved short-lived. He agreed and they resumed their relationship with a new intensity.

His last year at Kings Point was marked indelibly by the tragic assassination of the young President and the end of Camelot. Upon graduation in July 1964, Eddie eagerly returned to the sea, this time as a licensed Third Assistant Engineer and, after a relief voyage on the America, the iconic passenger ship, he returned to South Africa on the Robin Trent.

He also decided that he wanted to enjoy his newfound freedom to the utmost, so he allowed his five-year relationship with Sophie to end, more through neglect than any deliberate act. This he soon came to regret as the loneliness that accompanied long voyages from home had him realizing what she had come to mean in his life.

In 1966 he decided to come ashore to enroll in graduate school[19] and to seek her hand once more. But alas it was too late. Sophie had found another. Learning of her marriage sent Eddie into a prolonged period of despair and regret for what might have been.

But redemption was at hand. Her name was Patricia Burns and she was destined to be his loving partner for the rest of his life. Almost exactly ten years to the day he signed on to the African Star, Eddie and Pat were wed. In the ensuing years they produced a daughter Jeanine and a son Michael.

The years rolled by, bringing happy and sad times as one generation, the greatest one of their parents, passed on while another came forth in the form of grandchildren Michael and Catherine.

§•§ •§• § •§

Like a malignant disease that doesn't kill, but prolongs the agony and suffering of the patient, the apartheid regime in South Africa persisted well in the 1980s, despite international pressure and economic sanctions. It was not until Nelson Mandela was released in 1990 that apartheid was dismantled. Universal suffrage then resulted in his election as President in 1994. He was instrumental in ensuring that the transition did not result in black-white violence. The country remains a democratic oasis and as beautiful a place to visit as it was in 1961.

---

[19] In 1968 he earned an MS in Nuclear Engineering from Columbia University.

The Portuguese relinquished colonial rule of Mozambique in 1974 but, unlike South Africa, the story is a sad one. The country erupted into tribal civil war and armed conflict between Marxist revolutionaries and anti-communist factions. The struggle resulted in the death of thousands, with more than a million fleeing as refugees, and destruction of the country's infrastructure and economy. Even today the turmoil continues unabated – a sad lesson in what can happen to a stable country when suddenly abandoned by its colonial rulers.

§•§ •§• § •§

The thriving American merchant marine of 1961 performed one last act of greatness before it left the stage of history. Throughout the Viet Nam War, hundreds of American ships and thousands of seamen delivered millions of tons of supplies to the forces fighting in US uniform, as it did throughout WWII, in many of the same ships that served in that global conflict. But this was for an increasingly unpopular cause and, unlike 1945, the outcome was not victory, but withdrawal in 1975.

Change was coming, driven by technological and political winds which blew ill for the ships and sailors (now men and women) of the American merchant marine. Containerships made general cargo ships like the African Star and the ports that served them obsolete. Congress decided that the next war would not require hundreds of American bottoms to carry supplies to our forces in some foreign theater of operations. So the operating subsidies and route franchises that made lines like Farrell economically viable were withdrawn.

The decline was swift. By 1986 American flagged vessels were down to a handful and storied shipping companies, including the flagship US Lines, disappeared. Shipbuilding in the US became nonexistent for large merchant vessels.

Sadly, today a passenger, cargo or tanker flying the American flag in global trade is not just an endangered species. The American merchant marine is on life support.

§•§ •§• § •§

As for the African Star her remaining life story is a tragic one. After 1961 she remained with Farrell Lines but was shifted to an Australia - New Zealand route. In March 1968 with a full complement of 63 aboard (12 passengers, 48 crew and 3 cadets) she suffered a collision with an oil barge in the Mississippi.

SS African Star Following 1968 Collision

She was soon engulfed in explosions and flames which caused the deaths of two passengers and fifteen crew members, including two of the cadets from Kings Point class of 1970[20] who had just begun their sea year training. A truly horrific toll of lost humanity and a reminder of the hazards of serving in the merchant marine even in peacetime.

The ship returned to service for Farrell Lines after extensive repairs. She was later sold and, no longer flying the stars and stripes, her name was shortened to Star. In 1973, after twenty-seven years of service, she arrived at the scrap yard and then, was no more. One wonders if her DNA can be found in some other vessel or mighty bridge, built with her steel.

---

[20] P Hanley and D Nagele were Kings Point athletes who played fall sports and were embarking on their first Sea Year voyage in March 1968. May their souls Rest In Peace.

§●§ ●§● § ●§

Old age causes one to look back, as the future rushes implacably towards us. Much of it is yet unknown, but there is certainty regarding the eventual outcome.

The long ago events of 1961 described here are but a blink of an eye in a life now almost eight decades long. But their significance far outweighs their brevity and they provide a storehouse of memories to which *we* – my eighteen-year-old self and I - often return in the quiet of the night.

Made in the USA
Columbia, SC
03 June 2023

3583bd0d-1883-4f72-9370-1fba0789e00aR01